240

OUR
HEAVENLY
FATHER

Sermons on the Lord's Prayer

Harper & Row, Publishers

NEW YORK AND EVANSTON

OUR HEAVENLY FATHER

Sermons on the Lord's Prayer

by HELMUT THIELICKE

Translated with an Introduction by
JOHN W. DOBERSTEIN

OUR HEAVENLY FATHER
Copyright © 1960 by John W. Doberstein
Printed in the United States of America

H-N

This book is published in Germany
under the title of *Das Gebet das die Welt umspannt.*
Copyright © 1953 by Quell-Verlag, Stuttgart.

Library of Congress catalog card number: 60–11788

Contents

5

6   Contents

The great things of life
are bestowed only upon those who pray.
But we learn to pray best
in suffering.
—PETER WUST

Translator's Introduction

The first appearance in English of Helmut Thielicke's sermons has been greeted with the kind of response that calls for more, and *The Waiting Father, Sermons on the Parables of Jesus,* is herewith followed by another series which in his native country continues to be the most widely read of this author's many books.

The original title of these sermons on the Lord's Prayer is "The Prayer That Spans the World," but the English title is no less descriptive, for the mighty *cantus firmus* (as Dietrich Bonhoeffer would say) that sustains this deep-throated preaching of the Gospel is the theme of the Everlasting Arms that surround and enclose this creaking, frightening world. It is the theme of the heavenly Father, the universal answer to the universal need of man—his aching, though unacknowledged, homelessness and fatherlessness. This need is the recurring theme that haunted Thomas Wolfe in all that he wrote. He summed it up in this way: "The deepest search in life, it seemed to me, the thing that in one way or another was central to all living, was man's search for a father, not merely the father of his flesh, not merely the lost father of his youth, but the image of a strength and wisdom external to his need and superior to his hunger, to which the belief and power of his own life could be united." To that need the Lord's Prayer speaks and this is its soaring greatness. And it is not too much to say that it is the greatness of these sermons on The Prayer. Here, I think, lies the secret of Thielicke's preaching—his sure sense of man's need for a Father.

But the Lord's Prayer is not simply a great utterance of man's universal need. Thielicke never lets us forget *who* uttered the prayer, its particularity. Thomas Wolfe, we must conclude, looked in the wrong place and never found the Father. So life for him remained an "incommunicable prison." Men's search for the

Father finds its goal only if they listen to him speaking through his Word, which is Jesus Christ.

These sermons were preached some years ago (in circumstances related by the author in his preface to the reader, which should be read) and to people in a different land, but both American and English readers will readily supply parallels from their own situation and convince themselves that the fundamental human predicament remains the same. Because Thielicke lets the Gospel of God's seeking mercy and grace speak to this never-changing hunger, these sermons do not quickly grow out of date.

A recent commentator on the religious scene, who has kept his finger on the pulse of modern preaching, points out that all too much of it exhausts itself in "well-meant moralisms," seldom letting the "weight fall on 'Christ, the power of God and the wisdom of God.' "* Well, here is the antithesis, the antidote to all such tepid, eviscerated, emasculated preaching. Thielicke's preaching is preaching of the Word of God, which is always both judgment and grace, both Law and Gospel. Elsewhere in his published work I ran across a sentence that sums it up: The Word of God with its Law and Gospel is "like a starshell that lights up my life and shows it to be the valley of the shadow of death and also reveals the contours of the 'hills from which cometh my help.' "

Readers of these sermons will soon become aware that they are spoken, not merely written, addresses. Often an abstract, impersonal statement is made and then there is a sudden shift of point of view and the listeners are brought right into the midst of the situation. The pronouns become "we," "you," "me"; and "you" and "I" are immediately involved, engaged, addressed. This shift also occurs in tenses; suddenly the past becomes present, a shift which is disturbing to the orderly mind of the copy-reader. This characteristic of Thielicke's preaching (which he shares with Luther) is not merely a homiletical device; it grows organically from the preacher's constant urgent concern to communicate the living, contemporary Word of God to his hearers and readers.

Luther said that "the Lord's Prayer is the greatest martyr, for everybody tortures and abuses it." What he meant, of course,

* Martin E. Marty, *The New Shape of American Religion* (Harper, 1959), p. 146.

was that it is so familiar that we are constantly tempted to pray it mechanically and thoughtlessly. If my own experience counts for anything, I should say that no preacher can read these sermons on the Lord's Prayer without having his own preaching strangely warmed, deepened, and fortified, and no layman can read them without seeing that this Prayer must change his whole existence.

At the author's prompting, I have felt free in the translation to take occasional liberties with words and phrases, but I am not aware of taking any liberties with his sense. Again, as with *The Waiting Father,* I am happy to have a part in allowing this great preaching to be heard in English.

Mount Airy, Philadelphia   JOHN W. DOBERSTEIN
April, 1960

The Eternal is hushed and still,
The Temporal strident and loud;
Silently, over the strife on earth,
Moves the will of God.

WILHELM RAABE

To the Reader

These sermons, delivered to congregations in Stuttgart, were addressed to people who continued to assemble throughout the horrors of the air raids, the declining days of a reign of terror, and finally through the period of total military and political collapse and the beginning of the occupation. They were begun in the Church of the Hospitallers when Stuttgart was still more or less intact and its cultural life still flourished in the midst of war. They were concluded in the small auditorium of St. Matthew's parish house, the largest auditorium available at the time when there were no more churches in Stuttgart and only bizarre remnants of walls showed where the venerable Church of the Hospitallers once stood, where people had lived for centuries, people who had now come face to face with Eternity.

The preacher saw written upon the faces of his hearers the destinies from which they had come or which they were approaching. He sensed the tension they were feeling, not knowing whether the next moment the scream of sirens would scatter them in all directions—which happened not infrequently. He saw on those faces the torment of doubt and despair, the hunger and thirst for a valid comfort and

13

encouragement that would stand the test in hours of work, in hours spent in underground shelters, suffering agonies of body and mind.

All that the preacher read in those faces and also what filled him to the brim, since he too was a participant, is doubtless reflected in these sermons. And the Lord's Prayer was able to contain it all. There was not a single question that we could not have brought to it and not a one that would not have been suddenly transformed if it were put in the form of a prayer.

The Lord's Prayer is truly the prayer that spans the world: the world of everyday trifles and universal history, the world with its hours of joy and bottomless anguish, the world of citizens and soldiers, the world of monotonous routine and sudden terrible catastrophe, the world of carefree children and at the same time of problems that can shatter grown men.

The whole world rests in the hand of the Lord, like the golden orb we see in medieval pictures. And it also rests in our hands when we lift it to God in prayer.

What greater thing could there be than to learn to see this world in a new way—by starting with prayer?

The following sermons are an attempt to gain this new way of looking at the world. And to the author it seems important that they should keep in view a world in which the furies had been unleashed, a world that was forced to reveal itself—the actual world in which these addresses were delivered. This meant that any kind of phrasemaking and glorification of the world was ruled out. Here only the whole truth and the naked truth can stand; here only the *center* of the gospel message can make us free. And the fact that we have penetrated to this center we owe not least to the times of catastrophe on this earth. For he who "has" at such a time, to him "will more be given." But "from him who has not," even what he thinks he has will be taken away.

HELMUT THIELICKE

OUR
HEAVENLY
FATHER

Sermons on the Lord's Prayer

I

Our Father, Who Art in Heaven:
PART ONE

*And when you pray, you must not be like the hypo-
crites; for they love to stand and pray in the synagogues
and at the street corners, that they may be seen by men.
Truly, I say to you, they have their reward.*

*But when you pray, go into your room and shut the
door and pray to your Father who is in secret; and your
Father who sees in secret will reward you.*

MATTHEW 6:5–6

Some years ago a well-known periodical published
an article on prayer in which the argument went something
like this:

People must engage in something like prayer and for the following reasons. People today are being constantly assaulted
from the outside by so many things, like work, haste, tele-
phones, correspondence, the hooting and clanging of traffic,
the radio, and movies, that they absolutely must erect a wall to
protect themselves against this avalanche of impressions and
demands. The best way to prevent one's being completely
absorbed and devoured by these impressions and claims is
to enter into a state of inward composure which must con-

17

stitute a kind of counterbalance to our present way of life, which is so constantly turned outward. This state of inner composure, the article goes on to say, is undoubtedly similar to what the Christian calls "prayer." Naturally, when one engages in this inner soliloquy one need not act as if one were really speaking to a "thou," to "God." One must be quite rational about it and abandon this old resort to a "world beyond" where one's most secret thoughts are supposedly heard. One must quite soberly make up one's mind that this is really only a matter of talking to oneself for the purpose of clarifying and composing our minds.

What a tragic delusion, this yearning for prayer which denies itself any actual fulfillment! Behind the heroic, set face of this man lies the whole tragedy of a child who has lost his father.

For, after all, the real, inner situation that is reflected here can be described as follows. Man is walking through the dark forest of life in the gloom of night. Specters are lurking all around him and strange sounds disquiet him. The dark forest is full of dangers. Modern man calls this weird sense of threat and danger the anxiety of life, the fear of life itself. He would give a lot if there were someone to go along with him, someone who would put his hand on his shoulder and say to him, "Don't worry, I am with you. I know the pitfalls, I know the dangerous cliffs, I know where the robbers lie in ambush, I'll get you safely through. As long as I am with you nothing can hurt you." He would give a lot if this were so.

But now man knows—or thinks he knows—that this someone does not exist at all and that he actually is *alone* in the dark forest of his life. So he begins to talk aloud to himself, as children do when they have to go down the dark cellar stairs alone, comforting themselves with the sound of their own voices. But there is nobody there, and he is dreadfully alone.

Now look at this! Here is Jesus Christ teaching us, contrary to all the appearances of this life, that we really can say, "Our Father," and that there actually is a Voice that will answer us. But the truth is that I have reversed the proper order by speaking of *our* voice and the answering voice of the *Father;* for the Father's voice was there long before ours. It is like the story of Samuel in the Old Testament: I hear a voice calling my name and all I can do is to say: Here I am; now you have me! Now I speak to him who called to me first by my name, speak with him as a child with his father, telling him all things, great and small, that trouble me.

Having made these observations, perhaps what the writer of that article said may suddenly turn out to be far more serious than it appeared to be at first sight.

At first sight it would appear that this article was written by a man who is completely "unreligious," a man who has no religious sense at all and perhaps does not feel any need even to imagine a God who guides the world and rules our destiny. Perhaps he also has the familiar pride of the neo-pagan who simply refuses to recognize a God who is above him because he wants to manage his own life and likes to think of himself in the role of the sovereign strong man. So it may have seemed at first glance as I was developing the thought.

But there is another way of looking at it. What if the writer of this article were actually "religious"; what if he really did feel an urgent need to lift up his voice in the dark forest and cry out for his Father? But what if he were honest and sober and realistic enough to say that even so there *is* no Father in the dark forest of life, and therefore he must simply be brave enough to suppress this deep yearning of his heart to have a Father and to know that he was safe in his hands?

I ask you, isn't that a decent and honest attitude? I go further and dare to ask you this: Would even the very idea have occurred to any of us to expect a *Father* in this forest of our life—and especially in the ghastly valley all of us are going through in these months?

Doesn't the world seem a dreadfully "unfatherly" place when we think of the hundreds of thousands of graves in Russia, and the cemeteries of devastated cities? Can we help thinking of all those who sleep in those graves as orphan children, beset on every side by death and the devil, and without the protection of a father, children who sank into their cold graves before they had any inkling of what life can be?

Has it not always been so, ever since men have walked on earth; have they not always been terrified by the fatherlessness of the world? Perhaps mankind in its childhood dreamed of eternal, happy gods who filled Olympus with Homeric laughter and sipped the nectar of immortality. Even to this day our hearts leap—as in some bright, unreal suspension of our everyday life—when we read those ancient stories, but they leap as they do when we hear a fairy tale that transports us back to the unsuspecting days of childhood and for a few moments takes us away from the terrors of the world.

But this dream of reality soon changed and a harsher picture took its place. The more mature and knowing men became, the more they learned to know life, the more they realized how graceless, how fatherless, how terribly orphaned the world is.

The Greeks created statues of the gods that shine with light and seem to be reflections of their sense of a harmonious world. But we know today that this impression is deceptive. We know that these statues are no more than embodiments of a wistful yearning that lived in the midst of deep abysses and could not have endured existence if it had not been able to fashion that Apollonian dreamworld above the abysses. And the picture among our Germanic ancestors is not dissimilar. During the course of history their view of life became more and more knowing, more and more conscious of the encircling gloom. In late Germanic art the symbol of death and meaninglessness recurs with an almost tragic monotony in the form of the Midgard serpent that clasps the whole world in its dreadful embrace.

That is what the world looks like when we look at it with our own eyes. And all the carousing charivari in the world serves only to hide it from us and divert us for a while. Goethe, the so-called "Olympian," once said in his old age that he could hardly think that he had been really happy for more than a month in his whole life. And I believe that proportion would hold true in history as a whole: the happy times are like tiny islands in an ocean of blood and tears. The history of the world, taken as a whole, is a story of war, deeply marked with the hoofprints of the apocalyptic horse-man. It is the story of humanity without a Father—*so it seems*.

So the writer of that article would seem to be right when he intimates between the lines: "We are all orphans. We would like to have a Father, but everything in the world seems to indicate that we do not have one. But then I shall be honest and not act as if I had a Father. Accordingly, I shall let prayer alone and rather talk to myself, like a child in the dark, a child who fears the dark, but will not admit it, because this child is really being a man."

Of ourselves we can never arrive at the idea of being able to say "Our Father"; and even if we do hear something like the verse that says "Up above the starry vault a loving Father dwells," this may nevertheless leave a bad taste in our mouths, for we sense that someone uttered these words in an ecstatic moment when he was carried away by his own exuberance, seeing nothing but rosy skies and the goodnatured, loving Father enthroned above.

No, we cannot say "Our Father"! We really cannot!

Only on one condition—and that condition would be tantamount to a miracle—could we say "Our Father." And that would be if the Father had *first* spoken to us, if he had

revealed himself to us and we therefore had the guarantee
that he was actually and beyond all conjecture with us in
the dark forest and that when we cried "Father, Father"
we were not merely victims of the illusions of our own
yearnings.

And this is the point in our train of thought at which we
clearly see the tremendous importance that is to be attributed
to the fact that it is *Jesus Christ himself who teaches us to
pray the Lord's Prayer*. Remarkably enough, in this prayer
he himself retires into the background. And time and again
it has been concluded from this that Jesus himself had no
intention whatsoever of being the "Son of God," but wished
only to reveal the Father more clearly while he himself
remained unrecognized in the background, like an unknown
prophet, or at most was present in the way that medieval
painters included their self-portraits somewhere in the background of their pictures.

But now, suddenly we realize that it is fatefully significant
that *he* is the one from whom we received this holy prayer
of all Christendom. He is the invisible background of every
one of its petitions. All of them are nothing less than geo-
metrical loci that meet in him, even though he himself is
never mentioned.

For in him and in him alone did the miracle occur. In
him and only in him was the one condition fulfilled of
which we spoke: the miracle and the condition that the
Father should have spoken to us first, that he actually has
come to meet us in the dark forest. For this is the way the
Bible views the appearance of Jesus. The prophetic vision
sees him appearing against the dark background of night:
darkness covers the earth and thick darkness the peoples.
It is a world of pitilessness, of persecution, of loneliness, of
anxiety, a world in which God is far away. Not because
this is the way God made the world, but rather because a
rift runs right through it and the weight of guilt hangs
heavy upon it. Over all the world there reigns a night so

dark that hope seems quite impossible. This is the prophets', the Bible's picture of the world.

And here, against that background, we are given the *news*, no, not only the "news," it is actually *demonstrated* to us in the fact of "Jesus," that this hope nevertheless is there, miraculously and incomprehensibly there—and that the heart of a Father is beating for us.

Everything that this Jesus says, and what is more, everything he does is the reflection, the *reverberation of that heart*. Every one of his sayings is a pastoral, brotherly address. And this is what he says to us:

"You, my human brothers, live in a world of wounds and sickness and war, and I hear you complaining and quarreling with your Father and my Father. I hear what you are saying to him: How, O Father, if you do exist, how can you allow these things to happen? How can you allow cancer and multiple sclerosis and these endless rows of graves? You yourself made the blossoms—why do you blight them? Why should we believe that you are our Father? That's what you're saying, isn't it, my brothers?

"But look, don't you see that everything that torments you and makes you complain grieves my Father and your Father? *Your* sorrows are *his* sorrows; otherwise would I be standing here among you? He has sent me into the midst of your sorrows.

"Every wound I lay my healing hand upon has ached a thousand times in me; every demon I cast out has leered at me; I died the death that I myself defeated; I let my own body be torn and buried in the earth. Who among you suffers and I do not suffer with you? Who among you dies and I do not die with you? I am your comrade and brother in every pain, whatever your lot may be. Do you understand that? Then understand this too: He who sees me sees the Father, and he who sees me suffering with you sees the Father suffering. God suffers pain for you and with you; do you understand this?"

But even so there may be something in us that rebels against these words of Jesus. However comforting the thought may be that everything that wounds and torments us must first pass through the Father's hand, and, what is more, that he himself is wounded, that he too trembles beneath the blows that hurt us—nevertheless we still ask the question: Why then does the Father permit such things when he himself suffers from them? Why doesn't he utter his divine No and put a stop to them? After all, what we ask of a father is not that he should *feel* as a father does, but that he should *act* as a father should. Why does he let us go on only *waiting* for his kingdom in which, supposedly, there shall be no more suffering, nor crying, nor death? Why doesn't he stop this suffering, this dreadful crying in all the world, all the continents, and all the seas *here* and *now?* The "bird in the hand"—just a little relief, a little mitigation that were given to me now—would be better than "two birds in the bush," the kingdom of God, that uncertain future which we have to take on divine credit.

Haven't there been times when all of us have spoken in this way? But it is good to express our real difficulties with God's fatherliness frankly and openly. Indeed, it is part of his fatherhood that he allows us to speak in this way and does not reject us. It is part of the good news of the gospel that there is a Father to whom we can tell our doubts, even our doubt whether there is a Father.

I shall try, therefore, to trace the lines of Scripture that give an answer to the question. And I begin with a statement which is familiar to all of us.

There is prevalent among us Christians a manner of speech that manifests itself every time something terrible happens to us; it occurs, for example, in many death notices. "God, the Almighty, has taken away our son. God has visited cancer upon me. God has sent loneliness upon me." The idea back of all these expressions is that it is *God* who sends all these terrible things upon us: he not only creates the blossoms, but also the frost that blights them. He not only creates infants, but he also sends infantile paralysis upon them.

This is an utterly and completely unbiblical idea. On the contrary, what we hear in the Bible again and again is that the powers of sin and suffering and death are *hostile* powers, enemies of God. God did *not* will that they should exist. They are disorderly and unnatural powers which broke into God's plan of creation. They are the dark henchmen of original sin, our *own* sin. And just because these powers are hostile powers, Jesus' struggle against them often took on dramatic form. At the grave of his friend Lazarus, Jesus wept tears of mingled anger and sorrow. His spirit was angered by the dark powers that snatched away his friend and was grieved that these powers should be able to break into God's world since man through his fall has opened the door for them. And in the healing of the paralytic, Jesus again makes it very plain that the sickness which he healed is only the other side of the same derangement and disorder which sin brought into the world. All these things are signs of the disorder, the rift that runs through the midst of creation.

In the biblical view, it is actually an elemental law of human history that creation decays when it is separated from God. When God is denied and forgotten, men cease to understand one another; they know only too well that the other person is no longer held in check by the command of God, but is left to his own incalculable urges. And this breeds distrust, and distrust produces quarrels, war, fratricide. None of this did God will, none of it did God send. It is all the monstrous spawn and offscum of original human sin.

Indeed, even man's body is no longer an image whose likeness to God is immediately apparent; it too has been drawn into the great stream of disorder and downfall. Sickness and suffering are themselves signs of the rift that runs through creation. The biblical view of things can perhaps be expressed in this way. The guilt that we all share constitutes, as it were, a tremendous magnetic field and every-thing that enters into this field is drawn into this massive process of disorder and decay. And the connection between sin and the terrible convulsions that shake our tormented earth today forces itself even upon the minds of those who do not possess the full depth of biblical insight. And very often the connection is not with a definite, tangible, regis-trable sin, but precisely with this sin in the ultimate back-ground, the sin that lies behind every man ever born on this earth.

And now God allows this sign of the rift and disorder to hang above the world. He allows this history of sin and destruction, this disorder in his creation. And so it *must* be; he must allow it to go on; he must go on delivering us over again and again to our own fatality, for otherwise man, other-wise all of us, in our pride and our self-sufficiency, would forget the terrible abysses into which we have maneuvered ourselves without God. And haven't we in fact forgotten it again and again? Isn't it true that our Western civilization has seriously believed that it could live without God and rest on its own foundations? Are not even the most forgetful and the most self-sufficient gradually beginning to ask where this earthquake in the world of nations, this dreadful dis-aster of death and destruction, which no man can control, comes from? Are not even the pagans and worldlings be-ginning to be shaken by the anxious presentiment of the profound connections which may be at work in all this? Isn't it really true, therefore, that this sign of destruction and abandonment to the world's monstrous self-judgment must continue to stand?

It is true that the rainbow stands as a sign that God will never again drown the world in a flood, but will be patient. But it is also true that beneath it there is another bow, the bow of the curse, a warning mark of Cain on the brow of our fratricidal world.

We therefore must not simply say: "God" sends death, "God" sends cancer, "God" sends multiple sclerosis. The existence of these powers is radically contrary to God's plan of salvation. He allows it, and he undoubtedly is thinking his own higher thoughts when he does so. And even we men, small and sinful as we are, are sometimes able to grasp in our thoughts why God must perform this "alien" work, why he goes along with the world's judgment upon itself, and why he delivers us to it.

But then there is this other fact which is just as true— the totally new fact, which no man could ever discover by himself. Everything God permits the dark powers to do must *first pass in review before him.* Everything is examined and censored by his fatherly eye to see whether it will really work "for good with those who love him." Everything must first pass by him, every bomb that may strike me, every shell-splinter that may take my dearest away from me, every intrigue or chicanery that men may inflict upon me.

And since it must first pass by him before it can strike me, there happens what always happens when a thing or a person is looked upon by the eyes of God: a great transformation takes place:

Sufferings become trials which are meant to be endured in order that I may be purged and refined like the precious metal of gold.

The great times of terror, in which the furies of man's brutality, blindness, and *hubris* are unleashed, become times of visitation.

Death, the "last enemy," becomes the "desire . . . to depart and be with Christ" (Philippians 1:23).

The dreadful valleys of the shadow which I must traverse become the places where I learn to know the Good Shepherd and test his rod and staff.

The anxieties that torment me as I face the insecurity of my existence and the dark curtain of the future become the raw material from which I let God build my trust and my faith. "Crosses lift their arms above every pain."*

So we could go on at length, describing every conceivable terror, from the nights when the screaming bombs fall to the loneliness of war widows, from homelessness of thousands to the hopeless frustration of the soldier, young or old, who has been torn away from his job and his education, and despairs of ever finding his way back to normal life. I say that we can enumerate them all—and they are all evil things which are not in the Father's plan of creation—but we can also show how, or at least point to the direction in which, they are transformed when they pass through the Father's hands and how the mask of fate suddenly becomes the Father's face.

It is as if God intercepts these originally evil and disastrous missiles of fate, catches them in his fatherly arms, and sends them in the direction he wants them to go for the benefit of his children.

So everything is transformed for those who are his children, for those who have seen the Father in Jesus' life and death, and never again will let him go. *Then it comes from his hands; in any case it must go through his hands.* And we all know what a tremendous comfort it is to be able to accept something from the hand of God.

Even relatively light blows of fate become heavy when we cannot see that hand, and therefore they seem to be accidental, arbitrary, and meaningless. On the other hand, we can confidently accept even the hardest blows when we know that his good hand is at work in our lives. Then we know that, even though the sin and spite of men may be back of what may happen to us, even though men have tried ten times over to make it evil, nevertheless it comes from God's hands and because this is so, it has been transformed.

This gives new direction and new impetus to our lives. Now we don't have to ask what *people* were thinking when

* Reinhold Schneider.

they did this or that. We don't have to ask why fate permitted our dearest to be taken away from us. Now we are
free; free to ask another, more confident, question. And that
question is: What was God trying to do with us when he sent
this upon us? What is his purpose in all this? What are his
goals for us? We learn to look up, because God is a God of
purpose, a God with great fatherly plans for our lives, for
the life of his people, and the life of all mankind.

Out of the flood of thoughts that pours in upon us when
we say "Our Father" I have chosen and dealt with only one
in this first sermon. And this thought can be summed up as
follows:

Absolutely everything depends on this one fact, *that it is
Jesus Christ who teaches us this prayer.* He alone, in his life
and his death, is the guarantor that there is a Father, that
God is nevertheless at work in this cruel, hard, and fatherless
world, building his kingdom of mercy in the secrecy of the
Cross. So every sermon on the Lord's Prayer must of necessity
be a central preaching of Christ; otherwise it is romantic
fantasy, nothing more.

So let us praise him who enables us to say these "friendly,
sweet, and tender words," as Luther called them: *Our Father,*
and say them with honest, confident hearts. Only in him
can we ever know the secret that the Father's voice is really
and truly calling our name in the dark forest and that we
can answer as beloved children: "Abba! Father!"

Now everything will be all right, so long as we hear his
good voice calling to us above the howling of the wolves,
above the sound of branches snapping, above all the ominous
noises around us.

Now everything will be all right, so long as we answer him
and tell him everything.

Now everything will be all right and we shall be at peace
when *He* who accomplished it all walks beside us.

II

Our Father, Who Art in Heaven:
PART TWO

> *And in praying do not heap up empty phrases as the Gentiles do; for they think that they will be heard for their many words.*
>
> *Do not be like them, for your Father knows what you need before you ask him.*
>
> *Pray then like this:*
>
> *Our Father who art in heaven, . . .*
>
> MATTHEW 6:7–9

When a soldier on sentry duty hears footsteps approaching in the dark he shouts, "Who goes there?" This picture of a soldier on guard at night reflects our situation with God: in the midst of the enveloping night, in the darkness of this hopeless struggle of nations, in the shadow of our personal predicament and fears, again and again we hear a footstep; someone is passing by in all the thunder and the rain.

We do not know who it is. Is he an enemy or a friend, a power of fate or a Father? That's why we cry out, "Who is there?" We cry out into the night, in prayer as it were, "Who are you; who is passing by out there?"

"Who's there?" cries the young man who is beginning to look for the meaning of his life. "Who's there?" cries the young war widow who weeps in the depth of her pain and cannot believe that a Father would do such a thing. (But then, who is it that does it?) "Who's there?" cry those who are growing older and finding the riddle of life becoming more and more impermeable. "Who's there?" cry the thinkers who are searching for the ultimate common denominator to which the mysteries of life and history can be reduced.

They all cry out "Who's there?" for deep down they all sense that they would miss the central thing in life if they did not finally discover who it is that is passing by the sentry box of their lives out there in the darkness.

In the preceding meditation on the Lord's Prayer we have already learned how this whole situation is suddenly transformed, actually reversed, when we look into the eyes of Jesus of Nazareth. There we realize that we ourselves are the ones who are walking about in the vicinity of a sentry box; we are the ones who are suddenly being challenged. But strangely enough, it is not the usual sentry challenge, "Who goes there?" Somebody is calling us by name, as Samuel was called by God. So in this world there is an eye that watches over us, an eye that pierces the night and finds us in the dark. Somebody is there, calling us by name.

And now we must answer quite simply: "Here I am, for you called me. How did you know me? What do you want me to do?"

Then our prayer will no longer be an uncertain crying of "Who's there?" It will not be merely an uncertain response to some footstep of God or fate indistinctly heard in the dark of night. No, then our prayer will be a simple response to the call that comes to us.

God is always there first. God has always spoken first; long ago, before our little lives emerged from the deep darkness of our millennium-old chain of ancestors into the light of the world, Jesus Christ walked the earth, died and rose for us, ascended into heaven, and brought us to the Father. God is always there first, and therefore our praying is always only an answer to this simple given fact. Take Bethlehem and Golgotha out of the world, and the cry of God will be silenced and praying becomes meaningless. Then every one of us and our children and children's children are doomed all our lives to be lonely sentries in the lonely night, listening to furtive, disquieting footsteps, and never finding out who it is, and therefore obliged to cry out desperately "Who's there?" but never receiving an answer, finally to grow weary, return to our little sentry-boxes to sleep the rest of our lives the sleep of the hopeless, and drop the whole business of listening and calling.

Never can we realize too often this wonderful fact that a voice is calling to us from Bethlehem and Golgotha and the open grave, and that now our tongues are free to pray, so that now the note of praise and thanks may enter into our response: "Praise to thee, O God our Father; thou art the one who walks in the night and calls us. Now all is well."

In these words that introduce the Lord's Prayer, Jesus calls attention to still another aspect of the fact that God is always there before we pray. "Your Father knows what you need before you ask him."

This means quite simply this. When we ask God for something, when, for example, we ask for the healing of a sickness or for gracious guidance of our nation through all the present terrors, we should not think that we are bringing forward something new, for which we have to give special reasons or emphasis by saying our prayer more loudly and more vigorously. Long before we open our mouths God knows what's what. The very fact that God's eye finds us in the dark means that he finds our hearts, so filled with cares and desires, fears and hopes. He knows it all.

How does he know all our requests beforehand?

If we wish to answer that question, we must first state a very elementary but extremely important fact, and that is that we ourselves do not know what to pray for, and we do not know for the very simple reason that in the last analysis we know very little about our real needs, about what we lack and what we need.

When a person comes to a doctor, for example, with all kinds of fears and anxieties, he does so because he himself does not really know what he is afraid of. There is something vague and undefined within him, and this precisely is why he is so uncomfortable. The doctor must first bring out what it is, and the doctor therefore is more likely to know what is the deepest cause of the fears than does the patient.

So it is with our prayers to God (this is what Jesus is saying here). Often we ourselves do not know our deepest needs, and certainly we do not know what remedies we need. So we often pray for foolish things, when what we need is something totally different. We are naked, and instead of praying for clothing we pray for bonbons. We are imprisoned by certain passions, perhaps slaves of our vanity and our urges, and instead of freedom we pray for a Persian rug for our cell. So often we pray for senseless things that have no relation to our needs. And the reason is that we do not know the deepest wants and necessities of our life at all. And the psychiatrists and pastors know that it is precisely these unrecognized needs and secrets of our life that trouble people most.

What a look of liberation often comes over a person's face when you tell him straight to his face: "Your trouble is not at all, as you think, these other 'bad people' who are always making trouble for you, taunting you, and persecuting you. It's not at all the 'long run of bad luck' in your life that you can't get away from and keeps you thinking that you never get enough recognition, that everything goes wrong with you, and that people heedlessly pass you by. No, what causes all these troubles is nothing else but your own terrible need for recognition by other people. That's what keeps you on the watch to see whether every glance is an approving

one. That's what makes you measure your boss by the degree
of cordiality he shows, and get sore if he is even slightly
more casual than before. *That's* what makes you so terribly
touchy about your dignity when a subordinate gives you a
saucy answer."

I say, what a liberation it can be for a person when he
suddenly realizes that the real trouble in his life is not that
the whole world is opposed to him, but that there is this
unrecognized self-love! How stupid, therefore, it would be
for him to pray God to take this bad neighbor or this insolent
maid or this blasé boss off his neck! The sore spot is, after
all, somewhere else.

But this is just the reason why Jesus' saying is so thoroughly
comforting and true to life: "Your Father knows what you
need *before* you ask him." And we may add: The Father
knows what you need even *contrary* to what you ask. "You
can talk as you please in your prayers, you can chatter like
the heathen and argue like a lawyer, but not for one second
will God be diverted from the *one* theme of your life which
you keep evading; not for one moment does he lose sight of
the sore spot, the real need in your life, which, of course,
you don't like to talk about, because you would rather put
your fellow men on the carpet. It is true that it is not easy
to talk about; but this, too, your Father knows."

Jesus shows us that the Father knows our deepest needs
and secrets. And that means that he looks upon us men as
a mother looks upon her child who is sick or in pain. The
little child cannot tell what is wrong with him, and simply
looks upon his mother with great, appealing eyes. But the
mother knows what is wrong with him even though he cannot speak about it, and therefore she takes hold at the right
spot. As a father, as a mother pities her children, so the
Lord pities those who fear him and cry out to him in trouble,
even though it may often be the wrong trouble they are
crying about.

Here we can only cry out: Thank God that our prayer

does not depend on our expressing the *correct* desires, that it does not depend on our making a *correct* "diagnosis" of our needs and troubles and then presenting God with a properly phrased and clearly outlined prayer-proposition. Thank God that this is not so and that it doesn't need to be so, but that he knows us *before* we pray, that the Father is always there with his goodness *before* we come with our many words or with our great silences.

I can imagine that the paralytic (Mark 2), for example, had exactly the same experience. For everything that we have just described is here reflected in every word and act of Jesus. The paralytic's friends get him past the crowd and wangle him into the presence of Jesus by opening up the roof and letting him down. I can imagine that then all of them, including the paralytic, gazed at Jesus with a beseeching look, and that this imploring look expressed the prayer: Save him, save me from my terrible paralysis; save me from these signs of my own spiritual dissolution; make me well again!

But Jesus hears this unspoken prayer quite differently from the way they intended. He says to the sick man, "Your sins are forgiven," and thereby makes the point that the real trouble in his life lies in the fact that he is separated from *God* and therefore must necessarily be subject to his own passions and that with these passions he must necessarily come to grief. Here, at this point, lies the ultimate need of this crippled life. And that's why he needs first to be set straight *here*. Then, when that has happened, Jesus can also take away the sickness. The point is that Jesus knew what the sick man needed before he prayed for it—and knew that it was contrary to what he prayed for.

Moreover, this is also the reason why so many prayers seem not to be answered, though actually they are answered in a way that is totally different from what we asked for. The fact is that frequently enough the times when God seems to be silent or to deal with us in quite the opposite way from what we wished or prayed for are the very times when God's ways with us are most wonderful, and, of course, the most strange and amazing. For they are ways that are precisely in accord with what God has in mind for you and for me and what we need to reach his goal, and, of course, they are *also* ways that frequently enough are just the opposite of the goals we envision and pursue.

So these words of Jesus, "Your Father knows what you need before you ask him," contain a twofold comfort.

First, God is always there before we pray. The purpose of our praying and asking is not that we must scrupulously look after our own interests and be careful lawyers in presenting our own cause, in order that God may not forget this or that concern which means so much to us. No, the Father has a far deeper interest in us than we ourselves: we are his children, after all; we are Jesus' brothers. Therefore he knows all about it, and he can still make something out of our stupid, idiotic prayers.

Second, when God seems not to hear our prayers, this is not because he is indifferent to us or hard of hearing or even a hostile power. No, then the reason is that he knows our trouble and everything we need far more deeply than we ourselves, that he knows this as a father knows it, and that often enough he therefore prescribes quite different and more bitter healing remedies for our illness than are pleasing to our lickerish tooth and our terrible shortsightedness.

This is the comfort with which the Lord's Prayer begins, and this is the first thing we must understand when we begin to pray. Then the first thing we receive is a calm spirit, and we do not need to go plunging nervously and panically into a flood of words. Even in a bomb shelter, before we cry out to heaven that our house and our life be spared, before we try to forestall the onslaught of the screaming bombs by crying out, "Lord, help us"—I say, even in a bomb shelter we should say to ourselves quite calmly, "The Father knows, the Father knows. . . . He knows very well what is good for you in his plan for life and eternity, whether you go out this night homeless and robbed of every human security or whether once more it will all be given to you anew, whether you live or whether you are called to the ever-lasting home: The Father knows, the Father knows. . . . So, be calm and confident." Then in that calm confidence and peace of heart you can go on and pray.

Don't you think that then all of a sudden prayer becomes something altogether different, that then it suddenly ceases to be pagan chatter, and becomes the voice of a beloved child speaking with its beloved Father?

Your Father knows. . . .

But now I can imagine that some of you may object and say: "If the Father knows everything beforehand, this may well enough be a comfort, but then is there any sense in praying at all? Then isn't it superfluous? And all the more since it is so often the wrong kind of prayer? If God knows beforehand, isn't the only logical consequence we can draw that our praying is unnecessary?"

We shall deal with this objection for a moment because it actually leads us to the deepest meaning and purpose of all prayer.

The main thing in prayer is really not that we present particular petitions but that we enter into communion, into a personal relationship with the Father. If I do nothing else but say from the bottom of my heart, "Dear heavenly Father," the main thing has already happened.

But we know that even in human relationships speech is simply a necessary part of the fellowship. We all know, for example, of marriages in which the couples no longer speak to each other. Such marriages are dead relationships, bleak ruins of a love long since lost, even though they have not been divorced. A living relationship requires speech, the *word*, interchange. And when Walter Flex said that the depth of a friendship proves itself by the length of time one can be silent with each other without feeling that the silence is painful, what he meant was *eloquent* silence. This eloquent silence indicates a degree of fellowship in which there is a continuing interchange and intercommunication, but which no longer needs to be expressed in spoken words because the waves of an inner, inaudible conversation are constantly playing back and forth.

Because words and speech are an integral part of every vital, personal relationship, the Word is also central in the history of salvation. This is why Jesus is actually called "the Word made flesh"; for in everything that Jesus says and does and how he lives and dies God is speaking his Word into my life. And what he is saying is: You shall be my child; my whole heart is open to you.

That is why God did not merely give us pious *feelings* and subjective "religiosity," of the kind that is inspired by the odor of incense, the strains of sacred music, or the silence of a sun-drenched clearing in the woods. These pious feelings pass away, perhaps even within the next hour if some disastrous news should come to us. But the "Word" does not pass away. The assurance (and this means the Word): "I have called you by name, you are mine" is not something that applies only in the solemnity of a service of worship; it also follows us into the unsolemnity of a damp and cold bomb shelter or the consuming blaze of shuddering African skies.

And therefore the Bible does not say, as Goethe's Faust would have it, "In the beginning was the Deed," but rather "In the beginning was the Word." For deeds and doers pass away, and the froth and foam left by their passage through the ocean of history subside into the smooth surface of the water and scarcely anything is left to remind us of the spectacles that once created such great excitement and churned the depths of history. Again we say, the deeds and doers pass away! But God's Word, the Word that says he is our Father, the Word that has been calling out to us men from the first day of creation: "You are mine!"—this Word endures through all the eclipses of history; it sounds above the hoofbeats of the apocalyptic horsemen, and it will still be the saving Word on God's great last day of reckoning when the Judge will come to us and, suddenly, he will turn out to be our Father.

And note that we must also seek this fellowship through our "word," our speech. Only as we express in our own words everything that distresses us (the great and the little cares, the pressure of our guilt, our hunger for peace), only as we put all this into "words" and come before him, urging him, and saying to him: "Thou hast *said,* 'Seek ye my face' —look, here I am, seeking thy face; thou hast *said,* 'Cast all your anxieties on me'—here I am, casting them on thee; thou hast *said,* 'Knock, and it will be opened to you'—here I am, knocking; thou hast *said,* 'Whatever you ask in my name, I will do it'—here I am, asking; thou hast said all this, and now I come at thy *word*"—only as we come before him in this way will his fellowship be given to us, will we receive his peace.

In all this we learn something more: that the greatest blessing of this praying does not consist of our then receiving the specific things we have prayed for. (We have already seen that, for very deep reasons, petition and fulfillment can never be made to coincide.) We learn that the happy gift of prayer consists in receiving the fellowship of the Father, that he gives us his whole heart—*that we can accept everything from his hand.* That is why our will emerges from prayer quite different from what it was when we entered. It comes out a reconciled will, a will that leans on the Father and surrenders to him, in short, a will that sees everything that comes, whether it be love or suffering, as flowing from the everlasting, good hands of God, and therefore can say (not in sad renunciation but in childlike trust): "Not my will, but thine, be done."

Here is the point where we begin to understand why

we need the Word and why we need prayer if we want to enter into a living relationship with the Father.

And I believe that it is not too much to say that we can write the history of our country from the standpoint of the part that prayer has played and is playing now. We need to realize this one thing very clearly: When people stop praying, that is, stop talking *with* God and cease living and breathing in his fellowship, then all they are doing is talking *about* God. Then we merely discuss him and talk about the question of God. And the more we talk about him the more we break the thread and break down the bridge that leads us to him, however pious and serious these discussions may sound. Then it isn't long before we also stop talking "about" him, and more or less atheistically turn back to the order of the day. "You people who say you are interested in religion, why don't you pray?" The sigh of a dying man to God is more than a whole philosophy of religion; for in that sighing, stammering appeal the dying man is *alone with God*—and ultimately that's all that matters, whereas in a philosophy of religion, people are only *with themselves.* In our country, people are so dreadfully left to themselves because this has ceased to be a praying country. That's why the fields grow dry and our hearts are full of hate and the blessings melt away. When we lose our fellowship with God we also fall out among ourselves. The hands that hold the sword must also be praying hands; otherwise they wither away.

I cannot close without touching upon one last point. In the Lord's Prayer we all join together in one fellowship. We say "*Our* Father."

All of us who say this prayer together are very different. We are young and old, rich and poor, learned and simple; we belong to all races and ages on earth. But cutting straight across all these differences there is one single fellowship: we are all children of our Father in heaven. From our mother's womb we are all cast upon him (Psalm 22:10).

And in this company of children there is still another voice that is heard, the voice of him who called us his brethren and brought us back to the Father, so that now we can say *"My* Father," *"Our* Father." In other words, *Jesus prays along with us.* When our prayer is weak or listless or stupid, he lifts up our weak and tired words in his hands; and in his hands and on his lips they become true prayers. And when we stop praying altogether because we are beset by despair or the words die on our lips in our terrible spiritual loneliness (I am thinking of many of our Christian brothers in other lands), he never ceases to intercede for us. Jesus can understand even the sigh of the dying; he can clothe it with "beauty and glorious dress" and lift it to the highest rank of prayer. He who gave us this prayer prays along with us.

But he prays in a way quite different from ours.

We men must always compose ourselves and lay everything else aside when we begin to pray. The world, with its other gods and all its many cares and consuming desires, has become our home, and the region of prayer has become a strange and alien country. That is why it is often so hard for us to make the transition from our world to the realm of prayer. We are filled with cares, we are distracted and driven about by doubts and restraints. We stand at the bottom of the stairs, crying out from a long distance.

But Jesus lives and breathes in the atmosphere of eternity. For him, prayerful conversation with the Father is the familiar home to which he is constantly returning. For him, our native home is an alien place. Indeed, his sacrifice is that he comes to be with us in the far country. But he does it; he wants to be our brother.

So we cannot think of these "tremendous," "lovely" words, "Our Father," without remembering *him,* who came to be the Father's messenger to us in the far country and who now lets us share in his prayer and thereby makes our own prayers valid and fit for heaven. We should all be orphans were it not for him. There would be no one to hear us if he had not opened the gates of heaven. We should all be like sheep gone astray without a shepherd.

But now we *have* a shepherd. Now the gates of heaven *are* open. Now we *have* a Father. What can ever cast us down, what can ever unhinge us as long as we can look into that countenance and as long as we can say in the name of our brother Jesus Christ:

Abba! Father!

III

Hallowed Be Thy Name

But sanctify the Lord God in your hearts.

I PETER 3:15 (A.V.)

In one of his expositions of the Lord's Prayer, Luther made the disturbing comment on this petition: "I know of no teaching in all the Scriptures that so mightily diminishes and destroys our life as does this petition"; and to substantiate this statement he goes on to say that we all live a life in which God's name and honor are constantly maligned; we have other gods, and want to be masters of our own lives.

So underneath the surface, the first petition of the Lord's Prayer is a prayer of repentance, a confession of sin of crushing weight, and none can pray who does not pass through this court of judgment, this abyss of extremity.

For in every prayer there are two requirements:

First, we must know *to whom* we are speaking. And this is the very first thing that Jesus teaches us. We are privileged to say: "Our Father." Strictly speaking, this address is an unspoken, implied prayer of thanksgiving. If I were to put this prayer of thanksgiving into words I would say: "Praise to thee, O God, that thou art there and dost hear us. Thanks be to thee, that we may tell thee everything—from the greatest things our reason can conceive to the daily trifles that throng our life. Thanks be to thee, that we may speak to thee of our yearning for thy kingdom and yet of such small things as our daily ration of bread, which thou dost not deny thy children. Praise to thee, that thou dost let us pray in *this* way, that through Jesus Christ we are thy children."

This is the first requirement of all prayer: we must know *to whom* we are speaking—and it is to our Father, who hears us.

The second requirement that must be met and without which there can be no true prayer is that we must also know who *we ourselves* are. In prayer we not only appeal to the Father's heart, but we also beat our own breast. Nobody can say "Father" who does not at the same time say, "I come to thee from a far country and I am not worthy to be called thy son. Father, I have not hallowed thy name; I have betrayed it a hundred times."

Anyone who prays the Lord's Prayer attentively will see these two requirements fulfilled in every petition. Not only the first, that it is really the Father who is behind everything for which we pray, his kingdom which we inherit as his children, the daily bread which he provides in his fatherly goodness, and the forgiveness of sins which he assures us of day by day; but also the second, that in every word of every petition we acknowledge what we are ourselves.

"Father, thy name plays a miserably small part in my life. The name of my boss, the name of the men who are making history today, the name of my dearest mean more to me and engage me far more than thy name.

"Father, again and again I am unwilling that thy will be done. Even I, thy child, of all people, am constantly protesting and complaining whenever thou dost lead me in ways that are hard to understand.

"Father, 'I live in a hungry land without bread' [as Luther once said], and even though I am not starving myself, I live in a world in which millions are dying of undernourishment because the world has ceased to live in thy sight and share thy bread as children should."

We could go through the whole Lord's Prayer and indicate this note of repentance in every verse. In every petition we not only say, "Thou art my Father," but every petition mysteriously recoils upon us and God says to us, "You are the man" (II Samuel 12:7).

"It is because of you," says God, "that my kingdom cannot come. How can you expect to prepare the way for it when your own life is so full of roadblocks, barriers, and defenses against it, when you go on reserving certain monopolies in your life where I have no voice at all?

"You are the man," says God, "who is always trumpeting, 'Yes, Father, all this I will surrender to thee,' and then goes on secretly to say, 'Except this one thing: I can't use thy name in my business, I can't have thee in my sexual life. In this one area I want my own name, because this is the way I am or because life demands this or that of me in this area.'

"You are the man," says God, "who looks so little redeemed* that you go on spreading the poisonous seed of prejudice wherever you go. You, you are the man!"

The truth is that we cannot pray the Lord's Prayer to the glory of God unless at the same time we pray it *against ourselves.* And he who has not yet learned to pray this prayer *de profundis,* out of the depths of repentance, has not really prayed it at all.

For the fact is, as has already been suggested, that there are certain monopolies which we are determined to keep away from God, areas of our life which we are stubbornly resolved to keep for ourselves and which we refuse to surrender to God, areas of which we know perfectly well that

---

* The allusion is to Nietzsche's comment that Christians would have to look more redeemed before he (Nietzsche) would believe in their Redeemer. (Trans.)

God could never sign his name to them and which we therefore hide away in the bottommost pigeonhole of our life.

In every life there are these secrets, these dark documents
that bear only our own name, and to which God would
never put his name.

And this is, after all, our dreadful difficulty, that there
are these secrets in our life and that we will not dare to surrender them to God. Only a life that God could sign his
name to would be a free life, a redeemed life, a life at peace.
This is something that we must simply admit from the start.

Now there is one thing that we know of a certainty—and
even the most crass pagan may know it—and that is, that
there is no such life, that there never has been a life on this
earth (except the life of Jesus of Nazareth) to which God
could sign his name. And we know with equal certainty
that we shall never be able to bring it to the point where
it will be worthy of being signed by God. For the document
of our life is an IOU, a bond that shows what we owe and
never can pay. God could never acknowledge it with his
signature, his name.

And when I mention that word "bond," then we who
are not entirely unfamiliar with the language of the Bible
immediately read into it that totally new message that Jesus
brought to us, the message that this "bond" has been *canceled* and nailed to the Cross (Colossians 2:14).

Of course it's true, and nobody could seriously doubt
that God can never sign his name to our life. There is too
much in it that contradicts his name and defiles it. But now
God does something totally different. He does something
utterly new. He does something that we could never have
believed possible if it were not set before us so clearly in
Jesus Christ and if it were not sealed with his blood. He
allows the Son to declare in his name that in his eyes we are
now the brothers and sisters of our Saviour and no longer
vagabonds and rebels in a life that is lost.

And that gives the words "Hallowed be thy name" a completely new sound, an utterly undreamed of meaning that can be understood only if one knows Jesus Christ. Then the only way we hallow his name is to *recognize* it, to admit and confess with trembling and praise that the document of our lives is indeed a bond of indebtedness, but that in Jesus' name it has been canceled.

Then "Hallowed by thy name" no longer means: "I will see to it (with thy help, O God; and I pray for thine aid) and guarantee that my life will be cleansed and sanctified; I will endeavor and guarantee in future really to do what is right and fear no man; I will see to it that thou canst confidently sign thy name to it."

No, never again can we so interpret the words "Hallowed be thy name"; and all who have ever tried to interpret them in this way, from the rich young ruler to the moral idealists of our day, have been frustrated in their endeavor.

No, now "Hallowed be thy name" means: "Father, I will *believe* that thou hast canceled the bond; Father, I will *believe* that Jesus has paid the debt in full. Father, I will believe that now I can be thy child in his name; Father, now I really dare to pray, as little children are taught to pray:

'. . . Jesus, thy blood and righteousness
My beauty are, my glorious dress;
'Midst flaming worlds, in these arrayed,
With joy shall I lift up my head.

Bold shall I stand in thy great Day,
For who aught to my charge shall lay?
Fully through these absolved I am
From sin and fear, from guilt and shame.' . . . "

I shall stand! Bold shall I stand! I am back home again, back from the far country, with all my lost life and everything I could not cope with; and, behold, the lights of the Father's house are flooding out to meet me and I shall sit down in those festive halls to eat at my Father's table.

All that is what is meant by these words—now so mysteriously altered—"Hallowed be thy name." It means: "Out of the depths I cry to thee, but in these depths my Saviour is with me. I have no passport into the kingdom of God, attesting the blamelessness of my life, no papers to which thou couldst sign thy name. All I have is a bill of indictment. But thou hast given thy word and thy name that it has been canceled, and at thy word, and thy word alone, I believe that this is so. Jesus Christ said it. Jesus Christ has done it. In his name I was baptized and in his name I come to thee."

To say this and nothing else, and to glory in this—this is what it means to say, "Hallowed be thy name."

A petition that must otherwise terrify our hearts becomes the exultant shout of a child—a child who now can hallow the name of Father in no deeper way than simply to dare to call him "Father" and simply to accept the fact that the debt no longer exists. Christ is here, what can separate me from the love of God? Christ is here, what in all the world, from the devil to my own conscience, can accuse me and prevent me from being a child, from being called by the Father and welcomed to his home?

My friends, doesn't it strike you as it does me, that in the Lord's Prayer there is not a single petition that asks God to make me a sanctified, devout, and stoutly believing man, not a single petition that asks him to help me make progress in "sanctification"?

In making this observation I am not venturing to say that we may not pray for these things. Nevertheless it is striking that a petition that relates to the growth of the inner man and spiritual progress is simply missing.

Expressed in other words, whereas we would think that the Prayer could say, and quite rightly say: "Lord, lead me to further sanctification of my life," Jesus turns our attention away from ourselves, even from our pious selves, and concentrates it upon the Father. The prayer is not "May I be hallowed" but "thy name be hallowed." What does he mean by this?

Quite simply, he means to say that if I want to become a new man, I should not begin with myself, with my good intentions and my moral endeavors. This can only come to nothing, even though it is recommended by the philosophers, the moralists, and other honest people. For all these people have but one unanimous message to proclaim. They say that the only way to get anywhere is to do one's duty, to have ideals, and to try to be a good man.

Now I certainly have no desire to belittle these honest efforts. I know many honest idealists and many dutiful persons who could teach us Christians manners, and I take my hat off to them.

Nor did Jesus simply dismiss these earnest people who struggle to do their duty. When the rich young ruler, who was just this kind of person, came to him and told him how he had struggled and wrestled with himself and what he had accomplished—"all these commandments I have observed from my youth"—the evangelist's report of the Lord's first reaction was: "Jesus looking upon him loved him."

There is, however, one definite reason why this merely idealistic attitude cannot lead us to life. And I refer again, primarily in order to establish this fact as such, to the figure of the rich young ruler, who, as we know, came to Jesus after having kept all the commandments from his youth, and asked, "What must I do to inherit eternal life?" Let it be understood that he did not come to Jesus as a crass beginner in order to secure a bit of advice with which to make a start on a new life. On the contrary, he had already run the greater part of the race on his own strength, and somehow just because he had tried so honestly, it suddenly dawned on him that this would never do and that obviously he must change his whole life if anything was to come of it. What do you suppose is the ultimate reason why this kind of life which we propose to tackle and master by our own strength gets us nowhere?

The primary, main question of our life is whether we are

in fellowship with God. If this relationship of our life is right, then our interior life will also be right. No man can live inwardly if he cuts himself off from the source of life and retreats behind the frontiers of his own self in order to try to manage his own autonomous life.

When a man gets away from God he becomes like someone who is deprived of the sun and is therefore artificially isolated from the element of life which is a part of his nature. Then symptoms of decline immediately begin to appear because the life-giving element is lacking. This is a fact that can frequently be observed in everyday life; for example, in workers who are cut off for days from the sunlight or dwindle away in unhealthy factories, or even our brethren in the Far North. When this happens, a paralyzing weariness and listlessness settles down upon a man. He is literally cut off from the source of life.

So it is not surprising that he seeks artificial stimulants; he swallows caffeine, or he gives himself a lift with nicotine or a coke or vitamin pills. But the bit of specious life that he stirs up in himself in this way is only a delusion. In the long run he only becomes more miserable, and as time goes on his hangover becomes worse and worse and returns at shorter intervals—unless he leaps into the sunshine and restores connection with its life-giving rays, unless he goes back to his real destiny, which is to live beneath the sun.

And this is exactly what happens to the person who separates himself from God and goes into the far country where he hopes to be independent and run his life on his own steam. He runs away from the sun, to which he belongs by nature, and thus robs himself of its life-giving power.

Then he tries (he simply *has* to try) to get along with artificial stimulants. He whips himself up with ideas of duty, he submits to the knout of the eternal "Thou shalt," the scourge of the Law. He attempts to galvanize himself by pursuing great examples and ideals, or he may turn to some very cheap anesthetics and stimulants. The cheapest of these may be ambition: for example, the will to impress his fellow men at all costs, to put on a show and "be someone." So he tries to arrange everything he has as skillfully as possible in the show window of his life, and there can be no doubt that this passion for the show window can produce all kinds of exhibitionistic accomplishments that make people gape and gasp, "Oh, how wonderful!"

But we must realize very clearly that all these things are merely artificial stimulants.

Even the honest people who have tried this have found that they, too, get what I have called the "hangover" that comes from being deprived of the sun. They have found that they got nowhere, that something central was lacking. Why else should the rich young ruler have run up to Jesus and asked him what he was lacking, and why, in his quiet moments, he was always falling into that disillusioned, crapulent "headache" that comes to the moral activist. (For there can be no doubt that he had this "hangover headache," even though we could describe it more politely and discreetly by saying that he had come to a "critical point" in his inner life where he needed the help of a pastor.) And Jesus proceeded to tell him straight to his face: *"One* thing you are lacking."

And for all these people, it actually does depend only upon one thing, and that is to stop pumping up themselves and wanting to do everything themselves and to get back into the sunshine. Then their natural destiny would be restored and their lives would be given order and peace.

Dear friends, I believe that you have already seen why I have spoken at such length about this relationship of man to the sun. If Jesus does not teach us to pray, "Make *me* a consecrated, holy person," but rather teaches us to say, "Hallowed be *thy* name," what he is saying is this: "It doesn't depend at all on your own exertions and your own inner progress; you can never set yourself up as your own goal. Everything depends on your being willing to honor *God* and let him work in your life, simply to stand still and let him be the 'holy one' who will actually have first place in your life, above all men and all things. *Then the other will come of itself.* If you go out into the sunshine, or better, if you put yourself under the sun, you can be sure that these spiritual energies and blessings will also flow into you. This will happen all by itself and you won't have to go on goading and pushing yourself artificially with ideas about duty and the Law." Luther once spoke to this same effect, saying that one doesn't need to command a stone which is lying in the sun to become warm; it becomes warm—quite of itself.

Or don't you believe that a person who lets Jesus give him a living relationship to the Father actually does change even in his inner life? That a great joy comes over him because he is again connected to the primary source of his life? That his attitude toward the future is changed, that he stops worrying, and instead confidently accepts the coming days from God's good hands? That his relationship to his fellow man is changed, because he too is precious in the Father's eyes, and the Father loves him too? That his attitude toward the unsolved questions of his life, the question of guilt, for example, are changed, because he knows that none of these things can separate him from the love of his Father? Don't you believe that a person is changed on the inside when his relation to the sun is rightly ordered?

Again we say, the solution to the problem of our life (the problem of how we can become new men) lies not in ourselves but outside of ourselves, in the fellowship which we have or do not have with God.

The man who hallows God's name, lets him be his Lord, and surrenders his life to him will be drawn quite spontaneously and before he is aware of it into a great healing process, and he becomes a new person. A man cannot become a new person by deciding to become one. He can become a new person only when he allows himself to be incorporated into this living process of fellowship with God. *This* is the real meaning of our life, and the "new person" is only a by-product of this process. This is the order that must be observed if we are ever going to solve the problem of life and if we are to understand what Paul and Luther thought about (what they thought and taught, for example, about justification).

Quite in line with what we have been saying, Luther once said that a Christian is a man "who runs out of a dark house into the sunshine."

True, even Luther would not deny that a man who lives in the dark house of his own life, cut off from the sun, can force himself to laughter and hilarity. But he would immediately add that this laughter and hilarity are false and forced, that they are only a mask. It requires little insight to see that the great profusion of public amusements in our day are masks with which people for a few moments cover up their unhappy faces—faces that become more and more distorted in their unhappiness because of what is going on within. The soul of the man who sits alone in the dark house will be suffused with somber shadows while his face is screwed into an artificial smile. No man can produce that deepest joy by himself, and above all he cannot produce it out of his own inner spirit.

Only when he gets outside of himself will the joy come out from the inside, because it has actually come in from the outside—paradoxical, yes, but that's the way it has to be expressed.

> The Sun that smiles at me
> Is Jesus Christ my Lord;
> It's what in heaven I see
> That lifts my heart to sing.

Note that it is "in heaven," not in "me"! That is why I must come into relationship with heaven.

This is what Jesus means when he tells us indirectly that

we should not begin with our own holiness, our own moral advance, but rather concentrate our whole prayer on this one thing, that *God* may become holy to us, that *he* may occupy the ruling place in our life.

And here again we see how the deepest and most decisive question of our life can be, quite literally, reduced to one denominator and summed up in one name—the name of Jesus.

He is the one who brings me out of the dark house of my fatherless life. He—and he alone—is the one who tells me that the Sun is smiling at me, that God really means me when he says that henceforth nobody can accuse me, that he loves me, and that I need not be afraid.

He means me when he says: Your sins are forgiven. He means me when he says: Take up your bed and walk. He means me when he says: Don't be anxious about tomorrow.

The bond is canceled; the Son of God takes me by the hand; the Father is waiting for me.

Goodby, you dark, old house where once I lived. Now I know why you were so dark. Now I know, because now I know the light.

Thanks and praise to him who has done all this for me! Hallowed be his name!

IV

Thy Kingdom Come

Now when John heard in prison about the deeds of the Christ, he sent word by his disciples and said to him, "Are you he who is to come, or shall we look for another?"

And Jesus answered them, "Go and tell John what you hear and see: the blind receive their sight and the lame walk, lepers are cleansed and the deaf hear, and the dead are raised up, and the poor have good news preached to them. And blessed is he who takes no offense at me."

MATTHEW 11:2–6

Isn't there a comfort, a peculiar message in the fact that, after all the conflagrations that have swept through our wounded city,* a sermon can begin with these words: "We shall continue our study of the Lord's Prayer"? We don't need to interrupt and search the Bible for texts appropriate for catastrophe. The words of the Lord's Prayer are immediate to every situation of life. The farmer can pray it at the close of the day's work and let it wrap him round with the evening hush of its great tranquillity. The mother can

---

* This sermon was delivered in the choir of the Church of the Hospitallers since the church itself had been reduced to pitiful ruins in the air raids immediately preceding this time. The center of the city of Stuttgart was also totally destroyed.

pray it with her children in an air-raid shelter as the cargoes of death fly past overhead. The little child, experiencing the first presentiments of fatherly protection, the aged person, going through the trials and pangs of his last hour, both can say it.

It can be spoken by everybody in every situation, without exception, and we can see this with a special clarity in this hour as we gather together, a little bewildered remnant of the congregation, in the ruins of our venerable church, and begin quite simply with these words: "We shall continue . . . ," as if nothing had happened at all. For if we take eternity as our measure, what actually has happened? Is God any less the Father than he was before? Do the overwhelming events which have just happened have no place within the Message or are not these events themselves a message in which God sets his seal, in terrors and woes, in destruction and fire, upon what he has always been proclaiming in judgment and grace?

So we continue; the Lord's Prayer encompasses the whole world, and therefore it includes us too in this terrible exceptional situation of life in which we are all involved.

Our generation has learned to see the face of death behind people and things. When we meet a radiant, erect person we know with a tragic certainty that everything can change overnight, and we think of the refrain of the old soldier's song: "Ah, the roses wither, every one."

When we, inhabitants of a severely damaged city, walk through a flourishing undamaged section, almost involuntarily our eyes perform a little trick upon us and suddenly the intact façades are transformed into horribly mutilated walls and horror dwells behind the bleak and empty windows. We know what a house looks like beneath its sleek surface, and it is shockingly easy for our imagination to produce this little inversion in which the ordered system of beams are seen as a chaotic confusion of bizarre and splintered fragments of wood. Again and again the face of death peers out from behind the features of the living, and the shadow of ruins leers at us from the ordered peace of respectable homes. We are *cast upon the end of all things.* "All transitory things are but a parable," says Goethe, but now that we are really faced with transitoriness in the raw, the parable becomes too ugly and grotesque to be transparent.

In this world of death, in this empire of ruins and shell-torn fields we pray: "Thy kingdom come!" We pray it more fervently than ever.

We shall understand the full depth of this petition only if we remember that this kingdom is to be sought at the point where two lines of the Bible intersect.

The first line is a descending one, and it indicates that mankind is constantly living farther and farther away from God. Mankind began its journey in fellowship with God in paradise, which is, so to speak, the prototype of the kingdom of God. But immediately man's stubborn self-will asserted itself, and the departure from the Father's house ensued. What began as the protest of the individual, as individual sin, continued as collective sin in the building of the tower of Babel and took on the sweeping, tumultuous proportions of an avalanche. And if we are inclined for a moment to minimize this movement and assume that this is just a matter of human-all-too-human moral lapses, the history of idolatry in the Old Testament teaches us very explicitly that man in his self-seeking defiance has given himself over to the dominion of alien lords and tyrants, to whom he can surrender of his own free will but whose domineering, demonic grip he cannot shake off once he has crossed the boundary "beyond God." So this descending line leads us inevitably to the mystery of divine *judgment.* For God's judgment does not consist in his destroying the offenders with a thunderbolt from heaven; it consists rather in his leaving them to their own wretchedness and compelling them to pursue their chosen road to the end, and go through every phase of its terrible curse.

"God gives them up" (Romans 1:24)—he leaves them to themselves—this is his fearful judgment. There is nothing more terrible than the man who is left to himself. For all the instincts and energies which were previously directed toward God are now turned in upon himself, and he himself becomes the victim of his own self-seeking, his megalomania, the lie in his own life.

I believe that this characterization of God's judgment also provides the key to unlock the mystery of our apocalyptic world situation and also the mystery of the terrible visitation upon our own city.

In these fearful, fateful weeks many people appear to have become alienated from their faith in God; they begin to ask how he can "permit" such things to happen. It would be better, however, if they were alienated from their faith in *men*. It would be better if they were disabused of their fanciful faith in progress and stopped talking so emotionally and sentimentally about the "nobility of man" or the superiority of the civilized races. But since by nature it is obviously very hard for all of us to face this disenchantment, God gives us up to the foolishness of this drunken human delusion and watches us, reeling and staggering beneath the drug of idolatry, to see where it will lead us. Step by step God goes through the accounts with us, tracing the error to the end until even the blindest must see the bankruptcy he is facing. God leaves the rebellious man to his own consequences. This is the fearful form his judgment takes. And nobody can stop the deadly progress of this fate*; he must drink the drugged cup to its last dregs. Then perhaps he will learn again, and then really learn, what is good and what is evil. But then he will know it in a new way, totally different from the way he knew it in that primeval moment when he reached for the forbidden fruit.

So much depends upon our recognizing this form of

* The attempted revolution of July 20, 1944, occurred immediately before this sermon was delivered and was brutally put down.

judgment in which we are now involved. Only the Bible helps us to understand the present hour because the Bible knows the quintessence and the measure of every hour, because it knows the eternal.

Like all preachers, I have often felt compelled to preach repentance in recent years, but whenever I did so I felt as if I were a stormy petrel in a cloudless sky whom people refused to believe because they did not understand the signs of the times (and how could they when they were suppressing eternity and refusing to see the impending explosions?). They were eating and drinking, marrying and giving in marriage, and laughing at those who were building their arks in order to withstand the floods and the judgments. And I would assert that now that the floodgates of heaven are beginning to open and the great tribulations have begun, we Christians can breathe more easily despite everything, because after a great and oppressive silence God has again begun to speak even though it be in a voice of thunder. But the heavy atmosphere in which we waited for what was coming has cleared, and the speech of his wrath is easier to bear than his silence. Again we see God's plans being realized, and the more the plans of judgment are realized in power, the more may we hope that his promises and consolations are also in operation and that the Father is no less a reality than the Judge.

So this first line in the Bible is quite clear: it is a descending line of decay, a line that ends in the terrors of a world which is its own destruction, as is envisioned in the last book of the Bible and expressed in words of our Lord himself (Matthew 24 and 25).

But alongside of it there is another line. And this line is represented by the *coming of the kingdom* which goes on simultaneously within the other process. In the same measure as men turn away from God and go reeling on in the drunkenness of their own misery so God's dominion on earth mysteriously goes on growing on earth—even now. The manifestations of God's will are emerging ever more clearly and conclusively in the very midst of decline and decay, and God's sovereignty rules in power above all the rebels and usurpers, bringing his great and ultimate plans for the world to fulfillment.

We know very well that we must not think of this mysterious growth of God's kingdom (it really is a mystery!) as a kind of evolutionary development. We must not think of it as a gradual Christianization of the world which will increasingly eliminate evil. Such dreams and delusions, which may have been plausible enough in more peaceful times, have vanished in the terrors of our man-made misery. The nineteenth century, which brought forth a number of these dreams and dreamers, strikes us today as being an age of unsuspecting children. No, the coming of the kingdom of God takes place in a totally different way. In, with, and under the world's anguish and distress, in, with, and under the hail of bombs and mass murders, God is building his kingdom.

Perhaps we can illustrate this mystery in this way. I say "illustrate" because this is the only way we can set forth a mystery. We cannot explain it; we can only interpret it and follow out its main lines. *The kingdom of God is where Jesus Christ is.* But Jesus Christ always lingers in the darkest places in the world. John the Baptist had to learn this as he sat in prison, watching the collapse of all his previous illusions about the kingdom of God. He saw the judgment with great biblical realism, and he preached it with power. But, like many of his contemporaries, he doubtless thought of the kingdom of God, which was to follow the judgment, as an earthly, Messianic state of order and peace and prosperity. And now bitter disappointment crept into his heart, for this Nazarene, upon whom he had set all his hopes, seemed to be nothing more than a great preacher, only a man who practiced brotherly love. No cosmic revolution sprang up in lurid flames from the footsteps of this figure. He went his way like all the rest. And the dark, demonic powers were still lurking in their hiding places—or even openly irrupting in sores and pains, in death and suffering, in wars and disasters, whistling down like bloody scourges upon those who sought in vain to escape the darkness and the shadow of death. That's why he sent the despairing message: "Are you he who is to come, or shall we look for another?" And the answer he received from Jesus was: "The blind receive their sight and the lame walk, lepers are cleansed and the deaf hear, and the dead are raised up, and the poor have good news preached to them."

And what this message means is that the kingdom of God appears precisely at the place where there is blindness, lameness, leprosy, and death. It does not shun any of these things because it is too good for the slums and haunts of misery, because only the distant realm of a golden city, a city above the clouds is worthy of the dignity of God. No, the kingdom of God is the light that is ineluctably drawn to the benighted places of the earth where people sit in darkness.

So when Jesus was asked when the kingdom of God was coming, he uttered those enigmatic words (secretly pointing to himself): "The kingdom of God is in the midst of you," meaning "It's right here, just as *I* am standing here in the midst of you" (Luke 17:21). The people who were gathered around him cherished the delusion that the kingdom of God would be an earthly utopia where ease and comfort reigned. But if this were so, then surely it could not be in the midst of them. For they had only to look around at those who were standing there with them to see precious little of that kind of utopian ease. What they did see was the whole host of human misery: eyes speaking the dull speech of despair, bodies crippled and deformed, the furtive glances of the guilty, and always the callous insensibility that turns away from the neighbor in preoccupation with its own troubles.

And right here Jesus says, "Here, right here in the midst of this misery the kingdom of God has come. For *I* am here."

God came all the way down to those who were heavy laden
with guilt and misery. He squandered his whole heart upon
them. And look, he also has the power to change it all! The
kingdom of God is in the depths, and Christ is here too. One
can never draw God too deep into the flesh, said Luther,
and one can never draw the kingdom of God too deep into
the misery of this world. So it is measured by standards that
are different from ours.

If we compare the time before 1914 with our own, at first
glance we may probably conclude that then we were closer to
the kingdom of God than we are now. Apart from some serious
exceptions, but exceptions nevertheless, there was a certain
well-being, even a relative comfort among the nations, a
certain prosperity among the colonial peoples, and there
was peace. If one wanted to, it was really possible to live a
peaceful life in this world "in all godliness and honor"—
at least so we are told by the older generation. And even if
we deduct a certain percentage and attribute it to a tendency
to idealize the past, the remainder still seems like a dream
to us today. Apart from a few stormy petrels, people of that
time probably felt that they were already experiencing something of the "fulfillment" that seemed to be coming nearer
and nearer. For that was the time when belief in evolution
and "progress" was at its height. And today? Who can utter
the word today without getting a flat taste in his mouth? Who
can still believe today that we are developing toward a state
in which the kingdom of God reigns in the world of nations,
in culture, and in the life of the individual? The earth has
been plowed too deep by the curse of war, the streams of
blood and tears have swollen all too terribly, injustice and
bestiality have become all too cruel and obvious for us to
consider such dreams to be anything but bubbles and froth.
In the face of that seemingly glorious development, have
we not been hurled back to the bottommost rung of the
ladder? Where in this world, which is increasingly being
turned into a valley of tears, contrary to the plan of God,

can even the slightest trace of the kingdom of God be found?

And yet I am not telling Christians anything new when I say that we have learned more, and probably also experienced more, about the kingdom of God in the crash of air raids and the terrors of our cellars and underground shelters than those peaceful and almost utopian times of comfort and well-being could ever suggest.

Let me mention only a few of these experiences.

We know—surely we have learned it by now—that even the greatest creations of human culture are as grass that soon withers away. The mass graves that fill the cemeteries of our city in these days show the frailty of man, who is more powerful but also more suicidal than all other creatures. Even the forms and structures of the church sink and pass away. Here we are gathered in a ruin and here I am standing before you in my old army boots, because I no longer possess the proper clothes for services. But we do not say all this in any mood of skepticism or negative resignation. On the contrary, all these experiences have a place in the message and in the sermon only because they make us turn our eyes away from the passing and the relative to that reality against which the gates of hell shall not prevail and which moth and rust cannot consume. And if we are not deceived, our generation of death will have instilled in it by God a keener sense of what belongs to the transitory side of life and what has to do with God's eternity. Perhaps we are being given a new sense of proportion for what is relative, what are only liturgical trimmings and decorative accessories *and* a deeper awareness that in all these things there is hidden the rock of God, which for one man is the very foundation of life and for another a stone of stumbling, but which will abide in both of these capacities until the kingdom of God has come and the kingdoms of the world have passed away.

During these days and weeks in our city we have been led through the dark valley, and it does not appear as if our journey were at its end. But in the very midst of this valley of the shadow of death we have also learned to know the rod and the staff and the Good Shepherd himself. The person who has gone through the nights of bombing with his hand in the hand of God, the person who has said to himself when whistles and sirens were screaming and the noise and shaking was at its worst, "If we live, we live to the Lord, and if we die, we die to the Lord," that person has experienced what that hand of God means with a reality that he has perhaps never known before in his life and in a way that he cannot forget.

In times of peace our evening prayer has its deep, sustaining meaning. (How should we be able to live at any time without contact with God and without fulfilling his command?) And yet we all know how often our evening commendation to God's protection had about it something Platonic and unreal. After all, the police would take care of our safety; the Watch and Ward Society would see that the laws were upheld; we had first-class locks on our doors; ambulances and modern hospitals were available in case of a sudden attack of appendicitis. One telephone call would be sufficient to set a whole apparatus in motion for our protection. How easy it was to be tempted to make of prayer just a kind of extra insurance that had no ultimate validity. But now the telephone wires are down, the hospitals destroyed, the Watch and Ward Society is probably bombed out, and the doors are shattered. Luther spoke of God's right hand and God's left hand. With his left hand he governs the world through the ordinances of the world. And now he has suddenly removed his left hand, and we are committed with an unparalleled immediacy and exclusiveness to God's right hand. Now we have to reach out for this right hand of God and let it be the pillow on which we rest, the watcher at our bed, the guide on our dark and uncertain path, and our staff in the valley of the shadow. In the ancient language of the church, the right hand of God has always been a special symbol of his sovereign rule;

and have not all of us felt the touch of that power—precisely in those moments when God seemed to be delivering us over to the power of men and the forces of nature? Have not all of us had at least some awareness of that circle of protection that God draws around us, which the powers of evil cannot invade, not even in the case of those children of God who have perished in the midst of pagans, worldlings, and scoffers and in that circle of protection knew that they were still being called by name even in the last gasp of death? Many of the children of God believe that now the woes and terrors have multiplied so far that the kingdom of God is about to come. Is not this intensified expectation of the end itself an evidence of how God's rule grows mighty in the midst of terrors and makes men lift up their heads "because their redemption is drawing near"? *The greatest mysteries of God are always enacted in the depths;* and therefore it is the cry from the depths that always has the greatest promise.

May I tell you how I myself have come to feel and experience the reality of God's rule in these days of catastrophe, to feel it in all its mysterious hiddenness, and also in that hiddenness which is so oppressive that it almost reduces one to despair? At a time like this how can one speak at all except through personal witness and confession?

I have known moments—like everybody else—in which discouragement crept into my heart and I felt utterly stricken. My work in Stuttgart seemed to have gone to pieces; and my listeners were scattered to the four winds; the churches lay in rubble and ashes. On one occasion when I was absorbed in these gloomy thoughts I was looking down into the concrete pit of a cellar which had been shattered by a bomb and in which more than fifty young persons had been killed. A woman came up to me and asked whether I was so and so, since she was not sure who I was in the clothes I wore. Then she said, "My husband died down there. His place was right under the hole. The clean-up squad was unable to find a trace of him; all that was left was his cap. We were there the last time you preached in the cathedral church. And here before this pit I want to thank you for preparing him for eternity."

All of a sudden God had opened a door to his kingdom in the moment of catastrophe and in the midst of the collapse of the personal worlds of two persons. There it was between that woman and myself. I could not express this at the time, of course, because the words simply did not come to me. There are moments when we become speechless children. And God can take our very lack of words and make of it a praise.

That's how God can comfort; that's how he can let his kingdom come.

So God's kingdom really does come in all secrecy and hiddenness. Is there any more hidden setting than a bomb crater which is the grave of so many hopes, and also seems to be the grave of so many promises? God builds his kingdom in secret. It is like the building of a bridge that goes on beneath a covering of scaffolding, so that we cannot see the bridge itself, and we hear only the drumming of hammers. But one day the scaffolding and planking is removed and the bridge is revealed to our wondering eyes. God was not idle while we were looking in vain for the signs of his footsteps and his work.

But one day the hiddenness will be removed and the wonder of the works of God, the wonder of his dominion will be spread out before the eyes of all. Now God's rule is hidden beneath the Cross, and only he who accepts the Cross knows the secret. (What could you do with that bomb crater without the Cross?) But one day it will be made manifest and every knee shall bow—whether men fall to their knees in adoration or whether they are forced to their knees by the power of the Lord whose glory can no longer be overlooked. The moment will come when God will be "all in all." And that moment comes at the end of that hidden and seemingly tortuous road of the Cross where God seems to be nothing at all. This is our comfort in all our confused journeying—that it ends in glory.

Joseph Wittig once said that a man's biography should begin not with his birth but with his death. For a man's life is revealed only by its end, its goal. In exactly the same way it can be said that the secret of history is revealed only as we see its end. Actually, this is the way the Scriptures look at the history of the world; even though the first pages of the Bible start out with the very beginning of creation, they already include the end and the goal. For the intent of these pages is not to disclose where man came from but where he is going; their purpose is to outline the plan that God has for us and all the world. Therefore the real book of the secret of history is the Revelation of John. There the course of the world is revealed as seen from its end; there it ends in songs of angels and the redeemed; there the kingdom has come in all its fullness and immensity.

Already we are living in the name and the promise of that end; the lights of the harbor are shining in the distance, and we dare not think that God's little ship will ever go down before it reaches its destination. And while the angels are singing their praises, because the kingdom of God is in motion, it comes to us with power—to us who dwell beneath the angels' praise. Therefore: "Look up and raise your heads, because your redemption is drawing near."

V

Thy Will Be Done on Earth, As It Is in Heaven

Not every one who says to me, "Lord, Lord," shall enter the kingdom of heaven, but he who does the will of my Father who is in heaven.

MATTHEW 7:21

Every petition of the Lord's Prayer so far has taught us that it is a prayer that is uttered from the depths. I need only to recall to your minds a few thoughts in order that we may have this clearly before us.

When we look at ourselves, with all the pelting blows and burdens that threaten to break us down, we seem to be orphans delivered to the mercy of a pitiless and utterly "unfatherly" fate.* Not until we realize that we are encircled by the powers of fate—and all of us today know a little or perhaps a great deal of how escapeless they are—do we realize the tremendous liberating power that comes from being able to say: "Our *Father.*"

* The sermon was interrupted by sirens and an ensuing air attack. Shortly afterwards a second attack completely destroyed the part of the Church of the Hospitallers that was still standing, so that this was the last sermon to be delivered there.

And further, not until we consider that we live in a world in which men kill and die (and *how* they kill and *how* they die!), in a world in which we can fall into the terrible hands of men, a world in which only dim traces remain of the glory and the grandeur that God intended for his creation—not until we remember all this can we begin to measure the fervency of that petition, "Thy kingdom come," the fervency of hope and homesickness with which we await the coming of a new heaven and a new earth where God will be all in all.

And so it is also with the petition, *"Thy will be done."*

This petition too is prayed before the dark backdrop of a world in which, notoriously, this will is not done. Or are we to think that it is God's will that nations should exterminate one another, that churches and homes should sink into the dust? Are we to think that what we have experienced in our city and probably will have to go on experiencing is really God's will—not only what we now see as ruins, but, above all, what we do not see: the sad nights of the homeless and the bereaved, the mortal struggles and panics in the pits and cellars deep beneath the earth, the scenes of terror that nobody ever hears about—is all this the will of God? Or is not all this rather the will of the *men* who have done it or caused it to be done? Is it not therefore precisely that will which is in opposition to the counsels of God, that will which God has now given up to itself in order that it may vent its full fury and learn to realize the deadly direction which its own lostness is taking on the road to terror? (Compare the preceding sermon.)

But we do not even need to look *outside* of ourselves at all. Is all that goes on rumbling in our own hearts—the protesting thoughts that will not be reconciled, the fretful spirit of worry and anxiety, the egoism in our attitude toward our neighbor—is all this that goes on within us in thought, word, and deed, and even in our dreams, really the will of God? Is not this again our own will, which is so terribly hard to break and which never tires of arrogantly turning down the latch when God knocks on the door of our heart?

Is it not our own will that really makes us so unhappy? Is it not our own will that we want to be freed from when we cry: *"Thy* will be done"?

It's true; this petition, too, is a cry from the depths. And that's why it has all the promises of him who came down to us in the depths. This petition too plunges us into repentance, that hard but "godly grief" which, the Apostle says, leads directly to salvation, but which nevertheless is a bitter, dark corridor that must be traversed. For, after all, we should not have to pray at all that God's will be done, if it were really being done among us and if we ourselves and the whole world were not living our life in a constant boycott of his will.

Jesus makes it very clear to us in the Lord's Prayer that God's will is not being done among us. He indicates this to us through the peculiar form in which he bids us to pray that this will be done: that it may be done among us "as it is in heaven."

Obviously, what he means is this: May there be created here on earth the conditions in which the will of God is done clearly and unmistakably as it is among the angels of heaven who are constantly beholding the face of his Father (Matthew 18:10), constantly engaged in the heavenly liturgy, the unceasing worship of God. And as Jesus stands there saying this to us, there he is, the very figure in whom this heavenly fulfillment shines as in a mirror! For he alone was the one who could utter concerning himself that tremendous saying: "My food is to do the will of my Father in heaven."

Mark you, what he said was: My *food* is to do the will of the Father. It is not an "extra," a "dessert," which I think about only after the elemental physical needs of my appetite and my life have been appeased, something with which I round out the meal of life by giving it a bit of religious flavor. No, it is my food, it is the principal meal of my life to do the will of God. That is to say: Just as I live by my daily bread, just as my heart and my eyes and my whole body are driven toward food by the spontaneous urge of hunger, so I live by the will of the Father, so I am driven to him and linked to him with every fiber of my being.

Nor can we think of this tremendous self-acknowledgment of Jesus as being spoken with the slightest trace of Pharisaism, as if this total oneness with the will of the Father were a "merit" of his. He does not say this as if he were also saying: Look, how holy and noble I am to have been able to work myself up and refine myself to such a point! Look, that's how high I have lifted myself above my own nature and that of all the rest of you!

No, what he is saying is just the opposite: It is my *nature* to do this. In exactly the same way that it is a natural urge to be hungry and seek to satisfy that hunger, so my whole life is animated by a single impulse: to live in unbroken contact and complete harmony with the Father. And just as the stilling of hunger creates a state of satisfaction, perhaps even of blessedness, so I enter into a great peace when I live in this harmony with the Father. This is no merit, Jesus is saying, any more than the stilling of hunger is an accomplishment or a merit. It is an elemental urge of nature— though it is, of course, an urge of that unbroken nature which came forth from the hands of the Father. (Ah, my human brethren, what has become of your nature?) As for me, I would starve if I did not give way to my nature!

Dear friends, are not all of us such hungry ones? What strange creatures we are! We barricade ourselves within our own nature (our sick and altered nature), resisting the will of God and everything that he decrees concerning our life as if our whole happiness depended on our having *our own* will. Here is where a profound sickness and perversion appears: it is not only because of weakness that we men fail to do God's will, not only because we lack the necessary energy to obey or are too sluggish and give up too soon.

(This is how Kant interpreted human nature. He said that men know the norm of the good, the categorical imperative, but that they always fall short of that norm in their moral endeavors.) No, the sickness lies much deeper. Our standards of value have become so twisted and distorted that we do not *want* to do otherwise. This is not hard to understand. For example, our will constructs and pursues certain plans for our life. The more it does so, the more purposeful it is— and, after all, this is really a positive quality. We are determined, for example, to have a certain standard of living, we want to achieve success, we want our families to be happy —and if it turns out otherwise, we clench our fists and curse the will of God that spoils our plans or we fall into doubt and despair, and our love grows cold.

And all the while we are protesting, we grow more hungry and empty. For no man, no matter if he has tried it a hundred times, has ever yet found happiness in pursuing his own will.

This is also the way we must interpret that hour in Gethsemane in which Jesus took this sick will of ours upon himself and became our brother, struggling in the depths with his own will. Anybody who tries to catch the innermost pulsation in the heart of this story must come to the conclusion that when Jesus wrestled in a bloody sweat with his fate, the fate that would lead him to the gallows and utter bankruptcy, he was not struggling with God to make him accept "his own" plan for his life (insofar as one can apply the term "own" to the Saviour at all!). He was not fighting to be allowed to fulfill his Messianic destiny *without* suffering, *without* dying on the Cross. He was struggling in order that his own will should *not* get between him and the Father; he was struggling not to lose contact with the Father. And when that struggle finally ended with the words, "Not my will, but thine, be done," this again was not something that he uttered with clenched teeth—as it might be said by someone who has made superhuman efforts and still must capitulate against his will and then does so in the mood that says: There's no other way out, I have to submit; the will of fate has proved stronger than my own. No, that nocturnal struggler in the garden of Gethsemane uttered those words with a blessed sense of liberation: "Thanks be to thee, O God, that I may surrender my will to thine. Thanks be to thee that now I can throw overboard all my willfulness, all my own dreams and hopes. Thanks be to thee that I may renounce them all, and that now it no longer hurts me to do so, that it is really no sacrifice at all, but that I can cheerfully put myself in thy hands." There is good reason, then, that the story closes with the angel who comes to strengthen him. It is the hour of angels, the hour of communion with the world of glory, the hour of deep, mysterious, hidden happiness.

Nietzsche once said—touching, in his way, on the same problem: "You cannot endure it any more, your imperious fate? *Love* it; there is no other choice." It is precisely when we compare it with this pagan *amor fati,* this Nietzschean love of fate, that we see what an unspeakable comfort it is for a Christian to be able to say, "Thy will be done."

Nietzsche, too, saw that man simply grinds himself to powder inwardly when he constantly opposes his fate. We know this very well ourselves. For illustrations we need only to think of the many bombed-out persons who are simply eating their hearts out with bitter complaints, or the widows and mothers who have become a torment to themselves and others (on top of what is in all conscience hard enough to bear already) simply because they cannot reconcile themselves to their lot, and so they go on living in a consuming, nerve-shattering conflict with what has come into their life and cannot be changed. To all such people Nietzsche says— and here he speaks in the name of all men who are unredeemed but look at life with discerning eyes: Give up your opposition; you have no other choice. You will only ruin yourself. Try to love and to affirm what you hate. Try to love this enemy called "fate," since you cannot conquer him anyhow. Then at least you will regain your balance and your inner disruption will cease!

As if I could do such a thing—as if anything would ever come of it except complexes and an unnatural process of spiritual repression in which I tried to brush aside all the anxiety of fate and all my failure to cope with a smiling mask. This would be just like seeing a nonswimmer struggling for his life and crying for help, and then calling out to him, "What, are you afraid of drowning? Stop your futile kicking; love the water and affirm it." My guess would be that never yet has a life been saved in that way—because it would be crazy. But when it comes to the ultimate questions of our life, we men *are* crazy.

Again I ask: How can I love fate? After all, I can love only when I sense that there is a heart to respond to my love. The very reason that people suffer so terribly in their lives and because of the bombs is that with their human perceptive faculties they cannot feel that there is a heart back of it all.

And this is the point where we realize how completely Jesus becomes the pastor of our souls—in contrast to that will-o'-the-wisp comfort of the world which can give us no peace. For Jesus shows me that I can pray to my Father, that his will is done—even beyond my own prayer and understanding, and that therefore in prayer I can put my fate and my lot into his hands. Jesus does not ask me to do such a foolish thing as to love my fate. He never said to any blind or sick or lame man: You should love your sickness, your leprosy, your blindness; then you will stop groaning. Nor did he say to the mother of the young man of Nain: Love this terrible breach that death has brought into your life; then your nerves will calm down and your tears will be dried. No, he rather laid his hands upon the sick and tormented to show them how the Father feels toward them, to give them a sign that their pains grieve the Father and that he is present with his help.

And this is exactly what he is conveying to us in this

petition: "Thy will be done on earth, as it is in heaven."
What it means is this:

Everything that happens to you, whether good or bad,
must first pass muster before your Father's heart. Even in
the midst of tumult and war the thoughts of that heart are
thoughts of peace toward you. And if his dealings with you
appear to be utterly horrible, cruel, and incomprehensible,
then let your tormented gaze find rest in *me:* in my compassion, in my healing and helping that heart is speaking at its
clearest. Even the darkest places of your life must be seen
in this light, in this *Christ*-light. And only because you see
him there, only because there you see him as he really is,
can you love him—can you love him *in return.* Then afterwards, perhaps after long years of inner growth, you may
also learn to love and affirm what is now so bitter and cruel.
For the Father's hands transform and hallow the destinies
that flow through them. He who is reconciled to the Father
is also reconciled to his lot. For whomsoever the will of God
has lost its terror (and this it has for all who know the Father
of Jesus Christ), for him the darkest night of the valley of
life has lost its specters and it shines with light.

Now perhaps we have come far enough along to catch the
tone of joy and victory in the words: "Thy will be done on
earth, as it is in heaven." Those words were not born of
resignation and renunciation. It cannot be spoken by someone who merely capitulates to a divine decree upon his life,
from which there is no escape. No, there is something radiant
and shining about it: This prayer, "Thy will be done,"
is spoken to none other than the Father. And I can be sure
that if I let this will be done and if I hide myself wholly in
this will, this can only bring peace and fulfillment to my
life. For it is the will of him who stands before me here in
Jesus Christ and who has promised that with those who love
God everything works for good, and that where his will rules
everything comes out right in the end.

When this happens, or better, when we *let* this happen,

we are already joined to heaven and to the hosts of those who praise and love God in heavenly liturgies and whose food it is to do the will of God.

Not that this in itself will change this blood-soaked, pain-racked earth into heaven. Despite all the glory of creation it will always have plenty of dark valleys, narrow passes, suffering, and mourning and crying. Surely, nobody has to go to the trouble to explain that to us who are going through the most frightful of narrow passes right now. Nor shall we forget these hours in the depths if once more we should be brought to brighter heights. But above the darkness, heaven is open and the hosts of those who have overcome all opposition and now are perfected in undivided love look down upon us who are still marching on and contending with our lot.

And because we hear the songs of those who have become one with the will of the Father, we too begin to be comforted. The praise of the children of God in glory catches up our own pilgrim voices. It puts the bickering, complaining soul to rest and gives us, instead of gloomy resignation to our fate, a foretaste of the peace of God.

So when we say and repeat the words "Thy will be done on earth, as it is in heaven," this is nothing else and nothing less than a first, timid participation in the song of the heavenly hosts: Praise to thee, O God, that we can bury everything, yes, everything, in thy will, *our Father!*

VI

Give Us This Day Our Daily Bread

*Ask, and it will be given to you; seek and you will find;
knock, and it will be opened to you.*

*For every one who asks receives, and he who seeks finds,
and to him who knocks it will be opened.*

*Or what man of you, if his son asks him for a loaf, will
give him a stone?*

Or if he asks for a fish, will give him a serpent?

*If you then, who are evil, know how to give good gifts
to your children, how much more will your Father who
is in heaven give good things to those who ask him?*

MATTHEW 7:7–11

The Lord's Prayer embraces in its tremendous span
the greatest things and the smallest things. This vaulting
arch springs all the way from the prayer for the coming of
the kingdom, and thus the total transformation of all things
and every power-relationship, to prayer for our daily ration
of bread.

Great things, small things, spiritual things and material
things, inward things and outward things—there is nothing
that is not included in this prayer. It can be said by a child,

praying for bread and butter, and it can also be uttered in that agonizing zone between "annihilation and survival"* in which men fervently yearn for the coming of the kingdom which will resolve the hopelessly tangled skein of this world's conditions.

The Lord's Prayer is really a total prayer. And its seven petitions are like the rainbow colors of the spectrum into which light divides when it is refracted in a prism. *The whole light of life is captured in this rainbow of seven petitions.* Nobody can ever say that it sends him away empty-handed or that it does not take into account his need. It can be spoken at the cradle and the grave. It can rise from the altars of great cathedrals and from the dark hovels of those who "eat their bread with tears." It can be prayed at weddings and on the gallows. And the fact is that it *has* been prayed in all these places. All seven of the colors of our life are contained in it, and so never is there a time when we are left alone.

If the Lord's Prayer were not so familiar to us, if we had not so often looked through this prism, then surely this shaft of light that falls upon our daily bread would strike us as strange and astonishing. Is not this to talk about things too petty for prayer? Dare one come to God with such things without demeaning him? Is not this actually a trespass of materialism upon the refined realm of prayer, this sudden intrusion of the question of food and livelihood where only things "eternal" and "spiritual" should prevail?

I think that we ought to ask these questions quite seriously in order that we may then go on and re-examine our whole scale of values so far as our vital needs are concerned.

If we do this—and the "idealists" among us, especially, might well do this—we shall very soon discover that it is precisely the "little things" and among them our "daily bread," that

* After all the churches in Stuttgart had been destroyed, this series on the Lord's Prayer was continued in St. Matthew's parish house in Stuttgart-Heslach, where again they were repeatedly interrupted by alarms and sometimes had to be omitted altogether.

occupy a very high priority which is by no means lower than that of the big things in our life, for example, our interest in music or scientific and technical problems, or our profession or patriotic ideals.

A Beethoven symphony, which for many people may come close to being ranked as a divine revelation, sounds quite different if we have to listen to it when we are shivering with cold. And a visit to an art gallery is even less edifying (if at all) when we undertake it on an empty stomach without the fortification of "daily bread." Surely one of the blessings of our time (the hard experiences of which our generation must transmit to the coming generation when more peaceful times come) is that once more we have come to realize the importance of the "little things," the things we used to take for granted. There was a time when it would have been a sign of triviality, indeed, of lack of taste, if a person had ventured to compare the priority of a woolen sweater with that of a volume of Rilke's poems. Today we are not infrequently confronted with the hard and inelegant question of deciding which of the two to take with us into an air-raid shelter, and in these cold winter days it need betray no lack of "culture" when a person decides in favor of the sweater, and even certain journalists who used to write fine aesthetic criticisms of books and concerts are bold enough to advocate this choice.

Anybody who calls this "materialism" is only betraying that he has no conception of the part that "matter"—a warm stove, a woolen dress, our daily bread—plays in life. And then the additional consideration that perhaps 90 per cent of the lives of all of us (even the lives of those who are privileged to practice the so-called "cultural" professions, and therefore by no means only the lives of porters, street-cleaners, and others whose jobs confine them to little things) consists in "trivialities." Think of the little things that make a difference in our day that very often begins with a struggle against the Old Adam the moment the alarm clock goes off

—the hunger and weariness, the worry about how we're going to scare up a replacement for a broken windowpane, a roof tile, or a coal scuttle, the uncomfortable standing place on the train or a comfortable corner seat, the difficult letter we have to write, or the lovely letter we have just received. Is not all this something that occupies us far more tremendously and far more often than the grand and lofty questions or the "world-historical perspectives" which Spengler speaks of, on which, after all, these little things for the most part depend? To our shame, it must be admitted. But, shame or not, that's the way it is—and perhaps it's not a shame at all.

Now, just imagine that Jesus had forbidden us to relate all these things to our Father in heaven and to talk about them to him, simply forbidden it because they are too trivial for him, even though they mean so much to us. Imagine that Jesus had commanded us to speak to him only about the big things, like the kingdom of God, the world-dominion of Christ. the resurrection of the dead, and perhaps a few of those "world-historical perspectives" that open up in any assessment of the present total situation. If that were so, would we not be left terribly alone? Would not this simply leave the greatest part of our life fatherless, left to itself and relegated to cold loneliness? Then God would really be ruled out of our thronging everyday life and only a very small sector of our life would be considered worthy for God to dwell in. We would all be orphans, dear friends, if that were so. Only in our Sunday best and with scrubbed and shining faces could we dare to pay an occasional visit to our stepfather, hiding our calloused hands and the lines of care upon our faces. Then we should have to conceal from him all the little joys and sorrows of our life, only to find ourselves in the next moment terribly forlorn and alone again as soon as we were outside the stepfather's audience chamber, and everyday life came flooding back upon us with renewed force.

Thank God that it isn't so, that we do not have a "Sunday-stepfather," but the Father of our Lord and Brother Jesus Christ. Thank God that this Father is so compassionate and realistic that he appraises the little things in our life (including a warm sweater and our daily bread) at exactly the same value that they actually have in our life. Thank God that he accepts us just as we are, as living men, with great dreams, perhaps, and sometimes even with great ideas and achievements, but *also* with many *little* desires and fears, with hunger and weariness and the thousand and one pettinesses and pinpricks of life that fill even the lives of the great of this earth (one need only to read their memoirs).

But if you won't believe this—and it wouldn't be at all surprising, for no man could ever discover by himself the idea of such a fatherly and brotherly Lord; after all, all human ideas about God are much, much more sublime!—I say, if you won't believe this, then you have only to look at Jesus of Nazareth himself, who does not tarry in the broad dimensions of heaven but comes down into the narrow, straitened compass of our everyday life on this earth, into the very thick of things. And he whose eye encompasses in its boundless reach the first day of creation and the last hour of judgment, reflecting all the eternities; he whose outstretched arm enfolds the oceans, islands, and continents, because all authority in heaven and earth has been given to him, *he occupies himself with the trivialities of humankind,* with the grief of a mother who has lost her son (Luke 7:11 ff.), the predicament of a paralytic (Mark 2:1 ff.), the weariness of his disciples (to whom he says, Come, rest a while! Mark 6:31), and he does not fail to notice that the people who followed him into the wilderness are hungry. He is even concerned about the wine at a wedding (John 2:1 ff.). And he bestows his special love upon the seemingly worthless existences of those who are even more little than the so-called "little people": the lepers, the lame, and the mentally ill.

Truly, he knows not only the "kingdom of God," of which

he tells in his parables, but he also knows the people to whom he speaks about the kingdom. He knows, for example, that very often it is not the great ideas, the philosophical clichés and slogans that keep them away from following him and divert them from the kingdom, but rather that it is the little foxes that spoil the vineyards and the little carking cares that undermine the eternal foundations of our life. So the love of thirty ridiculous pieces of silver, or preoccupation with five yoke of newly purchased oxen (Luke 14:19), or an appetite for a pottage of lentils (Genesis 25:34) with which nothing could easily compete in the hour of exhaustion and hunger, so all these little things have always robbed men of their eternal birthright and blessing.

And just because the Lord knows man, because he knows his little desires and hungers, the blight of cares, pains, and thousandfold trifles that damp his spirit, and because he knows the almost equally numerous little joys by which man secretly lives, he comes to meet him right here, in the midst of his everyday life, and does not demand that man approach him only when he has screwed himself up to some kind of false elevation above the everyday things of life. He condescended to the depths of the stable to meet him. For even the external form of the Christmas miracle is connected with a "little thing" that the Lord took upon himself in order to meet us in the world of "little things," namely, the lack of hotel accommodations, the lack of shelter. We people living in a ruined city know well enough what such uninteresting trivialities mean for our life, and we are grateful to this Saviour for becoming our brother in the little things of life too, for condescending to our hunger and thirst and our shelterlessness (Matthew 8:20).

But as I say all this, I hear in my own thought and in yours an objection, which was given classic expression by the lieutenant in Walter Flex's unforgettable novel, *The Wanderer between Both Worlds.* There he says that one should really pray only for strength, that this is the only worthy way to pray—in prayer we should reach for the *hand* of God, not the *pennies* in his hand.

We are not unaware of the crucial truth in this statement, even though in this form it is very sharply expressed and only half true. Let us not despise the pennies and the crumbs of bread, if only because God's hand has condescended to include them *too!* The thing would be bad only if we wanted the pennies and the crumbs *without* taking the hand of the Lord. This is what the five thousand people in the wilderness did: they let themselves be fed, enjoyed the pleasant feeling of satisfaction, and then were off on their way. They looked upon the crumbs of bread and their full stomachs as ends in themselves. So they lost the meaning of the miracle of feeding as a sign, which was that back of it there was the *hand of the Lord,* the place from which all eternal and temporal goods come, the power that rules our life, the source of the grace in which we find our peace. That is why Jesus spoke out in sorrow: "Truly, truly, I say to you, you seek me, not because you saw signs, but because you ate your fill of the loaves" (John 6:26). And he could have gone on and said, "That's why the old humdrum 'Amen' you say after your table prayer sounds like 'Let's eat,' and the next moment you have already forgotten the little crack in the door which this small and insignificant bestowal of daily bread was intended to open in order to let you have a glimpse of the festal hall of the Father's house and your eternal home."

This bitter experience of Jesus is timeless in its truth, and he could say to us too (perhaps in these very nights when the bombs are falling): "You seek me, not because you want my divine protection, but because you don't want the bombs to hit you. That's why you sit in your cellars and whimper for a few pennies and a few more days added to your life— and when you get them, you have no more use for the hand that gives them to you. But then don't be surprised if this hand disappears more and more from your life and it grows more and more difficult to feel and to be sure of its comforting, fatherly pressure." (How often the despairing question, "Why does God hide himself, why is he so silent, where is God?" comes from this corner of our life.)

O you penny-wise, you crumb-seekers, why do you have so little faith? You go scrabbling on the floor—how unworthy! —for crumbs, when you might be sitting at the table as king's children, you keep your eyes glued on the floor when you might be looking into the shining face of your Father—and your bread will also be given to you *besides* (Luke 12:31).

But now that we have seen what Walter Flex means, the other side is also true: Now that we reach for the hand, we can also consider the pennies. A father who would not listen to everything his child says would not be a father. He may smile because the child so often has so little sense of proportion, because the child grieves more over a lost screw in his toy train than the destruction of his parental home, because the child has so little understanding of the difference between great and small things, but he listens nevertheless. God does not want only to be "praised"; nor does he want us simply to go on saying, "Thy will be done" and all the while, deep down under our own words, be tormenting ourselves because we have our own will and our own cares and troubles and are only suppressing them out of a kind of religious politeness which we associate with piety. Let us not fool ourselves: the Father knows what we are thinking. And so we can let out even our most secret desires. In other words, we should not only praise God; in this petition and intercession there is power and God has promised to listen (Luke 11:5 ff., James 5:17).

So we really do not need to pretend we are anything but what we are. We do not need to put on a show of being above the little and the big things in our life. God wouldn't believe us anyhow. This is why he also rejects work-righteousness and calls it hypocrisy, because this is only doing outwardly something different from what we are within.

But the person who acts as if all this did not matter to him, the person who thinks that as a Christian he must always go around with the shining face of a child of God, even in the hard moments of his life when he is stricken and smitten and the hand of God lies heavy upon him, always reminds me of a child who has gotten a rap on his fingers from his father and then says, "That didn't hurt me at all." We may and we should bow beneath what strikes us, and not ignore the school of God into which we are called. If we insist upon doing so anyhow, this does not lead to greatness of soul, but only to hypocrisy, to morbid, artificial cheerfulness, and inner complexes. In our relation to the hard blows of fate *and* in our relation to the little things of our life, we can come to God just as we are; and what we conceal from men (and should conceal) because of pride, we can say to *him*. But we are petitioners and we come with empty hands.

But maybe as we listen to this description of our relationship to God we are suddenly seized by a doubting question (for the great doubts always take us by surprise; suddenly they are there; nobody can ever lock them out; and now we must face them): *Isn't this a "small-minded" God?* Or are we not ourselves small-minded characters to come with such trifles instead of praying only for "strength" to bear our ordained lot?

In these considerations we dare not forget that it is God who takes the initiative. He tells us to pray this way. It is not as if we were forcing this talk about our little cares and troubles upon him; he wants us to pray to him about them. But everything that God touches with his Word and his command is mysteriously transformed. Luther frequently illustrated this by means of the water of baptism. By nature it is the same water the maid uses to cook with; in modern terms, it is H_2O. But when "God's Word is comprehended in the water" it suddenly acquires a dignity and becomes the bearer of the sacrament, and then it is something quite different from H_2O.

But if Jesus in this sense dignified even the lowly and little things and bestowed his words and miracles upon the wounds, the death, the cares, the hunger and weariness of men, then *we* should not act as if they were of no account.

The very greatness of God lies in the fact that he condescends so low. His *omnipotence* is surpassed only by *one* attribute: his love. And that love comes down to those who cry out for it, and his love is also there to listen to everything for which they pray.

Even in the case of an earthly king we usually do not feel that it is very "great" of him to cover himself with orders, medals, ribbons, and decorations. After all, we know that he has unlimited powers and we feel that he is only being cheap when he makes all too ostentatious use of it.

In exactly the same way we should feel that it was cheap and—in quotation marks—"divine, all too divine,"* if God were to clothe himself only with the glories of the rainbow and the setting sun, and had nothing else to do but celebrate himself in smoking mountain peaks and rumbling thunder. With an earthly king we have an even greater sense of his independence and sovereignty when he is able to condescend without losing his dignity. And this is God's way of condescending. Of course we praise him who holds the sun and the stars of the firmament in his hands. But for us he was at his greatest when the sun was darkened and as God he stooped so low that he took upon himself our human death in the death of the Crucified. Was it not always so in Jesus' life? Isn't it true that the very moments in the Saviour's life that are wrapped in hidden glory and flooded with the splendor of God's kingdom are those which are the poorest and seemingly have less than nothing to do with the King of the world coming on the clouds of heaven? I am thinking of the misery and the glory of the Christmas night, the humiliating and high hour when Jesus entered into the water of baptism with sinners, the squalid hour of betrayal when

* The allusion is to Nietzsche's phrase, "human, all too human." (Trans.)

the curve of his life turned and dropped in a sudden, sickening plunge, the very moment of which he could say (and *did* say just before it happened): "Now is the Son of man glorified" (John 13:31). This is exactly what the Romanesque artists of the Middle Ages were trying to say when they vested the Crucified with the insignia of royal dominion and placed the crown of triumph on his head.

In this lowliness lies the supreme greatness of God. And so it is with his attitude toward our daily bread. When we pray to him for daily bread and when we "little people" are permitted to talk to him about such "little things," this does not dishonor his divinity, but it does transfigure the trivialities. Does not this bread have a special dignity just because the Lord taught us to pray for it, because he himself took bread and broke it and gave it to his own? Does not there lie upon it the very splendor of the open heaven, the heaven from which the Father looks down upon all whose eyes are waiting upon him (Psalm 145:15)?

And just because of this splendor, this daily bread could be used as a vehicle and parable by our dying Lord, whose body is broken like daily bread and given to us as the heavenly food that we need, just as we need the daily bread on our tables.

Therefore the ancient Christians could never pray the Lord's Prayer without also thinking of this *spiritual* food— so exalted and filled with inner light was daily bread in their thinking; for was it not the *Father's* eye that rested upon it and *his* hand that gave this food to his children?

There is one last point concerning this petition that we should touch upon briefly. The Lord's Prayer teaches us to pray, not only for bread in general, but for *daily* bread, that is, for the "ration" that we need "today."

I have no idea how many pounds of bread are consumed in the average human life, and I certainly do not know how many tons of bread the whole of mankind will need to reach the day of judgment. But God does not ask us to pray for such quantities at all. He does not even want us to think and calculate so far ahead. Even "tomorrow" with its own cares (Matthew 6:34) is to be left in his hands; we are not to worry about what it will bring, but rather to cultivate the certainty that it does come from God's hand.

So Jesus takes this little piece of bread and, as it were, breaks it even smaller, putting only the portion for today into the Lord's Prayer. So low he bowed to little things, so concerned is he that we should learn to trust instead of calculating!

And he regards our spiritual bread in exactly the same way that he does our physical bread: his *Word,* which in parabolical language is called spiritual food, is not something that gives us complete directions for the rest of our life and a blanket consolation for every possible difficulty that may occur. No, we need his Word every day. His Word is a lamp to our feet and a light to our path (Psalm 119:105). You see what is meant; it lights each individual step, each step we take *now.* Only the next few yards are lighted by this lamp—no more than this, but no less either. This Word is not a searchlight that will bathe in light the coming months or years or even the course of this war and the years of peace to follow, so that we may see a straight road ahead of us. No, it is only a lamp to our *feet* and we walk like children in the dark because we hold fast to his hand. So in the spiritual sense, too, we receive only our *daily* bread.

We can entrust this present day to the Lord because the future and the last day belong to him. We can entrust the little things of our life to him because he is too big to concern himself only with what we men consider big (I Corinthians 1:18–31).

God be thanked that we can talk to him the way we feel, and come to him just as we are. We can cast *all* our cares upon him—*all* of them, not only the great and ideal concerns, but also the small and foolish ones. He will be able to make something out of it. But we must also aim aright so that we really cast them upon *him*. And therefore, *before* we speak of daily bread and the many other things, we must first say, and say from the heart: "Our Father!" The *Father* must always come *before* the things, but once this is understood, then bring to him whatever there is to bring. Because *he* has given you the greatest thing, *you* can come with the smallest things.

VII

Forgive Us Our Debts, As We Also Have Forgiven Our Debtors:
PART ONE

For we have not a high priest who is unable to sympathize with our weaknesses, but one who in every respect has been tempted as we are, yet without sinning.

HEBREWS 4:15

Among men there are sages and simpletons, scoundrels and saints, some who rule and others who are ruled. But straight through all these manifold differences there runs *one* common characteristic, and that is that every one of them —including you and me—must confess: We have all sinned and fallen short of the glory of God. Everyone has fallen short in a different way: the Pharisee falls short in a way different from the publican, the young man different from the aged woman. But all the differences meet together in that one sentence: "Depart from me, for I am a sinful man, O Lord." "We all came forth from thy hands different from what we are now; never can we give ourselves back to thee as we were when we came out of thy hands. All of us remain sinful

in thy sight. All of us have a great mortgage upon our life."
And that means "debt."

So when we pray this petition, "Forgive us our debts," we
do not pray it only for ourselves personally and individually.
In these words we bring to the Father the whole mountainous
burden of sin that weighs upon the whole world and like a
nightmare haunts this present historical hour. For this hour
in history makes us dimly, or perhaps sharply, aware that
back of its travails and back of the torments that have seized
and shaken the whole earth there stands a terrible sentence of
guilt.

So we come to the Lord with this petition as those who
declare their entire personal indebtedness and at the same
time vicariously acknowledge the guilt of the whole world,
the guilt of nations, governments, and all men. And we express this in one single, tremendously concentrated utterance
—in somewhat the same way that Jesus Christ on Calvary
gathered up the whole burden of mankind in one single,
mighty heave and loaded it on his shoulders.

We come as the ten "righteous," the ten undeservedly justi-
fied men in the Sodom of this furious world of ours and bring
before him our guilt and the guilt of the whole world. Wherever a Christian prays today he never speaks only for himself;
he always speaks vicariously in the name of all who are with
him in the far country—even though they themselves do not
know they are lost, and deludedly think this alien land is
their home.

In this our first meditation on this petition (which occurs
on the Day of Repentance) we shall confine ourselves to the
question of what is really meant by debt and guilt.

In the gospel, generally the terms "guilt" and "debt" are
understood not so much in the sense of an active breach of
God's command but rather as something that I owe and have
not paid, something that I have neglected and omitted
(Matthew 18:24, Luke 16:5, and elsewhere).

In the Last Judgment, Jesus Christ will one day confront

us with this indebtedness and will be obliged to say to us: "You did *not* feed me, you did *not* give me drink, you did *not* visit me (Matthew 25:43) when I crossed your path in the person of your hungry, imprisoned, lonely human brother. You owe me food, clothing, drink, attention."

And he might go on and say:

"I won't even mention the times you hurt your neighbor with hard words, heartless rebuffs, or malicious pinpricks, but only the things you failed to do.

"Do you remember the person you noticed because of the sadness that lay on his face, the person who was waiting for you to say a word to help him on his way? I can't find that word anywhere; it was never spoken.

"Do you still remember the soldier who was leaving for the front to face an almost hopeless situation? He shook your hand with a joke on his lips because he did not want you to see that deep down in his heart he was yearning to be able to take your last word with him as a blessing, an encouraging assurance. But you were preoccupied with other things; you had just experienced something nice or you were diverted by some banality or other. So you were glad the soldier made a joke of it because otherwise it might have cast a shadow upon your spirits and caused you a moment of suffering even to think of the abyss that he was going into. Now he is dead or missing. In all eternity I cannot find the words you said to him as he went to his death," says the Lord of the Last Judgment. "You must have failed to say them."

And there is your comrade, the fellow you work with, the quiet man in your shop, whose boss you are. He is a bit withdrawn and it is not easy to get next to him. Nobody pays any attention to him. Until suddenly it turns out that he is terribly unhappy, because something is wrong in his family or because he is naturally melancholy. And then you say, "How could I have failed to see what was going on!" and you are sorry you never said a good word to him.

How often in cases of suicide have I heard relatives and

friends say: I had no idea that anything was wrong with him. Why did we not suspect it? Because we had too little psychological knowledge or because our instinct failed us? No, it was only that we failed to love him. For no other reason. For love does not merely go into action with its help and support after we have learned that a need exists. On the contrary, love helps us to discover these needs. Goethe once said that one can understand only what one loves—and surely what he is referring to is not only botany and mathematics, whose mysteries never reveal themselves if we approach them with aversion, but rather the living person, the neighbor, whom I can understand only if I love him. Love, when it is really present, not only helps us to heal wounds but above all to discover wounds. This is why the profoundest understanding is also associated with a mother's love. A mother understands her child before it can say why it is crying, perhaps even before it cries at all. She understands her child, not because she has studied all phases of the theory and practice of child care, but because she loves it. Tell me how much you know of the sufferings of your fellow men and I will tell you how much you have loved them. Every time we fail to see the secret and perhaps consciously concealed suffering of another person we hear the Lord of the Last Judgment saying to us: "You failed to love him, otherwise you could not have helped knowing it. For love is expressed not only by the helping hand but above all in the eye that is quick to see. I have looked in vain through all eternity for your quick-eyed love. It must not have existed."

So when the gospel keeps telling us that Jesus knows what is in man and therefore understands him and sees him through and through, the reason is that he loves him. Perhaps the only reason that we can bear the thought that God sees through us, indeed, that he sets even our secret sins in the light of his countenance (how terribly hard it is for guilt to come out from behind its veil of secrecy!) is that we know that here we are not dealing with such a theoretical attribute of

God as his "omniscience," with the frightening specter of some gigantic heavenly intellect that nothing escapes, but rather that he loves us so infinitely. *That's* why he understands us so thoroughly. It is not the knowledge of a grand inquisitor who watches our every move and emotion, and enters them into the heavenly books, No, it is the knowledge a father has of his erring child. It is the divine love that nothing escapes because it is concerned and moved by everything that happens, because it sees not only the sin but also the homesickness of those who are living in the far country.

When Psalm 90 speaks of these secret sins which God sets in the light of his countenance, what is meant is everything that I have *not* done—the many fateful situations in the lives of my fellow men which I helped to create by doing nothing about them, the wounds I did not see, the cries for help I did not hear, the fears I did not feel, the despair that did not move me. And *I* go blithely on my way, for I am not conscious of any sin; after all, what have I "done" that was bad? If only it were something downright and massively bad that I had done, if only I had been cold (Revelation 3:15 ff.)! The terrible thing is that I am *not* cold, or rather, that I persuade myself that this is only my goodnaturedness and my good character, whereas perhaps I simply do not have the nerve and the vitality to be really bad and I go my easygoing, well-tempered, lukewarm way. For who can say that I have done anything wrong? I have always done what was "right."

But woe to us when in the light of eternity, the appalling light of God's countenance, there rise up against us the deeds unborn and undone, the unseen sorrows, the bodies suffering in the dark, the secretly straitened souls by the side of our life's road, whom we did not see but passed by, like the Levite on the road to Jericho.

Then we shall ask in amazement *why* the Lord of the Last Judgment should cast this in our teeth. "Lord, when did we see thee naked, hungry, and in prison? And if we had seen, we would have pitched in and lent a hand." Then the Lord of the Last Judgment will answer, "You did not see because you did not love. You loved too little, that's why your eyes did not see."

I should like to give another illustration from the catastrophic historical situation in which we are now living which throws a very special light upon this fact of our indebtedness. In any case, when I speak of it, it is not my purpose to make a "private" confession which concerns only myself and thus would be, as it were, a bit of autobiography. My purpose is rather to acknowledge and express a difficulty that we all face.

It always seems to me that one of the darkest spots in our dark time is that we are so overwhelmingly beset by the misery of thousands of refugees, mass graves, anxieties, shattered lives, that we have all become hard and insensitive, so much so that we are no longer conscious of our own hardness. A death notice which formerly would have troubled us for days we lay aside with a fleeting pang and go back to our work— simply because there are too many of them. We can no longer grasp the vastness of the suffering. It is like the ultrasonic tones which we no longer hear, or better, like a loud bang that shatters the eardrum and automatically shuts off the function of hearing. All of us are living in the presence of an ultrasuffering which is constantly moving farther beyond the limits of comprehension. And Jesus was speaking of this moment of ultrasuffering when he said that the increase of affliction causes even the love of the faithful to grow cold (Matthew 24:12). Even when we want to be faithful, we have no use for love, as it were, because love lets us understand too much, and too much understanding makes us sick, because it brings suffering too close for comfort. So we mobilize all our defensive energies and try to meet it by growing hard, or rather, this happens of itself in what is an almost automatic act of self-preservation on the part of our spiritual organism.

And because we armor ourselves against being hurt repeatedly, as our armor grows thicker our debt of sympathy for our tormented world grows greater. But if we have developed this hard shell toward the great world, toward the whole of its suffering, how much more serious this becomes when we are faced with individual cases, the torment of a mentally ill person in our family or the cancer our neighbor is enduring. Compared with the thousands of prisoners, what importance do those "few" disciples of Jesus have who are languishing in concentration camps and prisons for the sake of the gospel, suffering an anonymous and invisible martyrdom which is so fundamentally different from that of the medieval burning at the stake which is our usual image of martyrdom? We can hardly find a place in our hearts and minds and prayers for all this because we are already so occupied and consumed by the totality of misery all around us. We live in a time of over-crowding: the trains, the stores are overcrowded, everything is overcrowded—including our hearts. And this is the worst. How many people can we not think of, how many persons and things come crowding into our hearts! And added to this is the fact that we do not even know what the lot of many who are in need is like, and therefore cannot pray with any clear conception of their situation. Who knows anything about the real situation of his friends in East Prussia or in prison camps? Who really knows all about even *one* such case, which for-merly would have filled the newspapers with horror stories?

But enough of that. We are not going to wallow about in what torments us in all this and what perhaps in a few years from now we shall hardly understand. What we want to know is how he to whom we pray the Lord's Prayer and in whose name we speak it will help us. And the fact is that the very preponderance of the suffering that surrounds our life like a sheer wall can help us to find the only possible way out of this plight, this eternal incurring of debt and remaining in debt and never catching up.

In any case, it is of no use—I want to speak of this first because I see so many taking this wrong way out—it gets us nowhere when we try to soften these hearts of ours, which gradually grow harder and more insensitive, by constantly recalling some isolated scene of horror and nameless suffering and forcing ourselves to look at it. (The sight of it suddenly bursts upon us when we are celebrating a birthday, a wedding, a reunion or just sitting comfortably together—something that continues to happen occasionally *even* in these mad times. Suddenly the gray horror that lies on the margin of this festal evening creeps in, and suddenly someone becomes its spokesman, conjuring up the darkness: I wonder how so and so is feeling now. . . .) This constant gazing at the scene of sorrow, which we think is the part of love and duty, can only lead to inner illness and fruitless melancholy.

No, the only help lies in "looking to Jesus." The sufferings of all the world converge in him. His eyes reach out to the farthest corner of the earth, wherever there is suffering. He hears the sobs of the lonely and those bereft of every tie of family and possessions. He is wounded by the dread of the dying and those in mortal peril. He hears the sighs of prisoners behind their bars and electrically charged barbed wire. He bears upon his shoulders the cares that are cast upon him every hour and every minute from every square mile of the inhabited earth. He does not merely see this whole confused world situation in the large; he is not content with the divine perspective of a total view. No, he comes, as he did in the days when he walked the earth, to the individual, to the nameless one who lives forsaken in some back alley. He knows the little cares of children and the grisly hallucinations of the insane that no word can describe and no heart can understand. Yes, he also knows the joy of life in a sparrow and the exultation and the trembling fear of little creatures that live their lives far beneath the level where we human beings pursue our interests.

Could human eyes endure the sight of this vast sum of distress and gloom, of mutilated bodies and mortal dread? Could human ears bear the cries of misery that rise to heaven day after day and night after night?

And because he not only registers it but hears it in love, it wounds and hurts him. His heart is pierced by every knife that is drawn, by every bullet that is shot, by every evil word that is spoken. The Saviour is literally riddled with the suffering of the world.

Only so can we ever understand his suffering, and his suffering *with* the world. For he does not simply sit back "behind the line" in heaven, receiving toned-down reports of horrors on the world's front. Nor does he see it from the tremendous distance of heaven from which everything looks so small and insignificant—like a flier who sees the destruction of a city from a height of several miles, unable to discern the little things and the individual things: the mother who clasps her child to her breast in mortal terror, the bombed-out wretches, the crashing of sanctuaries where generations of men found their way to eternity. No, Jesus sees it all as if he were right there, as in truth he is. Through his incarnation he was himself delivered over to death and pain, to the cruel hands of men, to imprisonment, nakedness, hunger, and homelessness. "I was [really] hungry, I was [really] naked, thirsty, and lonely, not merely 'symbolically.' I took upon myself everything that overtakes you or ever can overtake you. Truly, I am your high priest and I can sympathize with you because I suffer with you."

So all the roads of misfortune converge in him and all the deadly arrows lodge in his breast. In every cellar that shakes with detonations he is a guest. In every troop of straggling refugees the Saviour trudges too—as he has for ages and will continue to do until the last day.

So there is one thing that is most emphatically true: when we are overwhelmed by the world's suffering and forget our debt to our neighbor, when our sympathy is hardened, then we should not allow ourselves to keep gazing at the horror in order to whip up our sympathy. Nor should we withdraw from it all and keep looking for ways to forget it. Rather in the midst of overwhelming suffering we should remember the *suffering of the Lord.* As we remember *his* poverty we remember all the poor; as we contemplate *his* imprisonment every prisoner is present in our thoughts; as we consider *his* death we help all the dying. *His suffering is vicarious for all.* And everything we do to *him* we have also done to the least of his brethren. And everything we have not done to him we also have not done to our brethren.

So Jesus helps us in several ways through this sense of continuing indebtedness. (In part two of this sermon we shall see how he helps us through his forgiveness.)

For one thing, he helps us by letting us see his loving and sympathetic understanding, in other words, by letting us see his Cross. When we hold *his* hand we hold the hand of *all* the suffering, afflicted, and imprisoned. For the sum total of all suffering is stored up and ever present in him.

And—be sure of this fact!—this is no mere Platonic idea that concerns only our personal edification, something that remains only in the realm of our inner life. No, this is something utterly real; for as we contemplate his suffering and his great mercy, our own hardened hearts are softened and in a very practical sense become receptive to all the suffering of our fellow men far and near. Because we see Jesus reaching out to the tortured and tormented, the insulted and injured, we can not do otherwise than reach out to them too. He who stands beneath this Sun himself grows warm. He who stands beneath this Sun cannot help but radiate light and warmth. So Jesus Christ helps us to pay our debts and replenish all we owe to our brethren.

Or better and more precisely expressed, it is really *his* compassion that takes our place; it is *his* power that helps us in our weakness. "It is no longer I who live, but Christ who lives in me" (Galatians 2:20). And in exactly the same way every man who learns from Jesus to love and understand his brethren will have to say: This is not *my* work at all, not *my* character, *my* empathy; this is the Lord himself, who has drawn me into his own vicarious suffering. Then he will say: I "love," and yet not I, but *Christ* "loves" in me.

So we can bring to him our hardened hearts, and he will melt them. So we can bring to him our love grown cold; he will love in our stead. But this is precisely the way he draws us into his own loving, and also kindles our love. Everything that is brought into his presence is healed and made whole. So we can also bring to him all our helplessness in the face of the world's suffering, which is so immense that our prayer and our sympathy can no longer cope with it. He understands even *this* helplessness and draws into the mighty stream of his eternal, high-priestly sympathy. And these helpless prayers, our terrible indebtedness and shortcoming, are in good hands when we leave them to him, for then they have been committed to that heart in which all the suffering and terror of the world is gathered up and endured and shared in love. And that poor, helpless sob comes back into this unhappy world transformed into a blessing and a mercy as the moisture of the seas and streams rises up to the clouds and returns to earth again as fructifying rain and dew.

So the Saviour can take even our helpless groans, even the things we failed to say and do or even to pray, and make something of them. He is the transformer of all things and all hearts. Out of his fullness he can give abundantly even to those who are far gone in debt, and the poor in spirit he makes partners in his royal kingdom.

So this is the law that always operates in the life of the Christian man: The longer he lives in Christ's discipleship the greater grows his poverty and indebtedness. But the riches and abundance of his Lord *also* grow greater and greater and make up for all he lacks. He must decrease, but his Lord must increase. And this he does far more abundantly than all that we ask or think.

VIII

Forgive Us Our Debts, As We Also Have Forgiven Our Debtors:
PART TWO

Then Peter came up and said to him, "Lord, how often shall my brother sin against me, and I forgive him? As many as seven times?"

Jesus said to him, "I do not say to you seven times, but seventy times seven.

"Therefore the kingdom of heaven may be compared to a king who wished to settle accounts with his servants.

"When he began the reckoning, one was brought to him who owed him ten thousand talents; and as he could not pay, his lord ordered him to be sold, with his wife and children and all that he had, and payment to be made.

"So the servant fell on his knees, imploring him, 'Lord, have patience with me, and I will pay you everything.'

"And out of pity for him the lord of that servant released him and forgave him the debt."

MATTHEW 18:21–27

The word "guilt"* makes us prick up our ears these days.** We all know that this word does not refer primarily to little moral lapses like not doing our duty or occasionally using strong language.

It is not a matter of peccadilloes or "puppy-sins," as Luther called them, and perhaps when we speak of guilt today the primary accent is not even upon the sins of commission and omission in our private, personal life. My guess is that today the first thing we think of when we hear the word is the world's guilt.

Are not all of us troubled by the question of who is to blame for the boundless misery of our time? Is not this the topic that engrosses us all whenever a few come together? Conferences on this question are held by statesmen, economists, and military experts all over the world, and the first thing they say is: This or that person or thing is to blame for the global catastrophe. And then we proceed to build all our plans for a new world upon this fact, namely, the "other fellow's guilt."

Was not this the case in the First World War? Surely everyone of us still remembers the watchword "war-guilt lie," on which men then thought they could build a new world—and hence a world which would be founded upon the "other fellow's guilt" and therefore would inevitably fall apart.

We all sense that somewhere in the hideous disaster which has befallen the world there is a great and terrible guilt. If only we knew *who* was to blame! The thoughts of all men in all countries today are like those of zealous policemen on the lookout for the guilty one. We moderns no longer make penitential processions and offer atoning sacrifices in order to blot out some hidden sacrilege which we dimly surmise behind the disaster, as the ancients did when the plague struck or conflagrations destroyed their homes. But we too have the

---

* Here the word *Schuld*, which can be translated as "debt," "guilt," "sin," "trespass," etc., necessitates a choice that fits the context. (Trans.)

** This was the last sermon delivered in the "Third Reich," immediately preceding the occupation of Stuttgart.

dim presentiment that there must be some terrible sin and sacrilege in our world when we see it hurled into such agonies and torments and when people begin to say what hitherto would have sounded to them like a strange saying from an alien world: "To the mountains, 'Fall on us'; and to the hills, 'Cover us' " (Luke 23:30).

Now of course there can be no doubt that there are war-mongers and therefore some who are guilty in high degree. But at the same time we also divine that when we are dealing with a world event of such elemental proportions as this apocalyptic war, we cannot saddle the burden of guilt upon any individual or group of men, as if all we had to do was to put the handcuffs on a few criminals and their cliques in order to restore the peace of paradise to humanity. For today we sense that something is wrong with our world itself and therefore this cannot happen. Somewhere in the background of this world there must be a terrible rift that is cracking its foundations and precipitating recurring catastrophes and breakdowns. For millenniums (actually since this world began) there has been a creaking and cracking in its framework. One crash follows another, wars and rumors of wars fill the air, and all the schemes and plans for a new world order, all the attempts to compute and establish a balance of powers are of no avail.

Where does this rift lie?

I have just said that we men are always looking for the guilt in others, not only in our personal life but also in the life of the nations, and that, for example, after the great wars the peace treaties are always based upon the guilt of the other side, and that therefore they always have the character of a peace of revenge and thus evoke a fresh desire for vengeance. This is the avalanche of guilt that keeps swelling and growing in the history of nations—and not only in the life of nations but also in the life of individuals. It can happen even in an apartment house. One party has some fault to find in another and lets him know it. The other party reacts accordingly. The principle of retaliation goes into operation: You hit me and I hit you, and the petty offense (perhaps only an unswept stair) swells and condenses into a poisonous atmosphere that can settle down upon a house, upon whole clans (Corsican blood feuds!), and whole continents. So the endless screw of guilt goes on turning, generating retaliation that leaps from one pole to the other and back again.

So the strange fatality in our human life and the life of nations is that it is always basing itself on the other person's guilt and forgetting to beat its own breast. And our world will never find peace, neither nations nor individuals in their private and vocational lives will ever find peace as long as only the cry for vengeance is heard among us and as long as we are not ready for reconciliation: Forgive us our debts!

And there is the key word to what Jesus is teaching us here. He does not teach us to pray: Avenge the guilt, O Father. Thou seest the injustice and thou hast the power to strike down the transgressors. Thou knowest the guilty ones, thou knowest the tormentors of our tortured world. The scourges that fall upon our backs, are they not thy divine scourges? Why canst thou not break them in pieces and cast them away, for now they have become guilty as thine instruments? Canst thou not rid me of the competitor, the one associate, the one tenant, the one person who has shattered my life?

No, Jesus teaches us no such thing. He absolutely refuses to be the spokesman of this voice of our blood and our natural instinct. Instead he teaches us to say: "Forgive us our debts." And the fact is that he does not intend this to be merely a private, devotional prayer. No, when I pray these words I am bringing into the light of God's countenance the guilt of all the world, war and rumors of war, every conscious and every unacknowledged wickedness.

But when we put it in this way there are two things to be remembered.

First, that in all the fateful guilt that hovers over the world, its continents and seas, *my guilt* is a part of it too. What I see

there is my own heart blown up to gigantic, global proportions; retaliation is the law that rules *my* little life too. I
know how very much I am merely an echo of those around
me. When people are kind and friendly, *my* face lights up.
When they vex or cheat me, my mind and spirit is darkened.
We need only to look around us to see the spark of malice
leaping furiously from pole to pole, in a crowded train, for
example, or in a queue outside some store or office, where
a single manifestation of spite or impatience immediately
flashes out and affects the whole group.

Second, I must therefore begin with myself and my own
guilt whenever there is anything to be said about the world's
guilt. I cannot simply look out the window and be morally
indignant over the great Babylon that lies spread out before
me in all its godless darkness. No, what I see out there in
global proportions must only remind me of my own "Baby-
lonian heart" (Francis Thompson). And quite involuntarily
I will be reminded of the prophet Nathan's hard rebuke to
David: "Thou art the man!" I am the one who needs forgiveness, and the sanitation of the world must begin with me.

Of course it is true that the commandments of God have
something to do with the preservation of the whole world and
the restoration of the nations to health. But it would be foolish to think that they are therefore a kind of world constitu-
tion which needs only to be correctly adhered to in order that
we may then go on living quietly and undisturbed "in all
godliness and honor"—as if we could live up to them! After
all, this is precisely the problem—that we cannot simply hand
out the commandments to the nations and expect them to
obey them to the letter in the same way one obeys the instruc-
tions of the civil code. If this were so, then there would have
been no need for Christ to die.

That is to say, one can keep the commandments only if one
has been placed in a totally new and personal relationship to
God. Only as we experience the fact that the Father loves us
can we fulfill the commandments with all our heart and all

our soul, and love God in return with all the strength of our mind. After all, we cannot love someone who is a stranger to us or who may even appear to be a hostile power of fate. Only as we know him who first loved us can our hearts be kindled to love, to a loving response. And furthermore, only as we learn in communion with Jesus Christ how he discovers the child of God even in the lowest of the low, how he sees through the layer of dirt that covers Pharisee and publican and prostitute alike, and dies for them all, only then are we too enabled to love the brethren, and their lives become sacred, even though they are vile and evil or mad and mentally ill and "unfit for life." When a person does not see men the way Jesus saw them or when a whole nation banishes this view from its midst, then there can be no more regard for others, and there can also be no more justice and certainly no love. Then human life ceases to be worth even a farthing, and the guillotines begin to operate full speed.

Some poor fools say, "The greater one makes God the smaller man becomes—until finally he becomes so small that he considers himself a worm." This self-depreciation, they say, is typical of the Christian way in which man approaches the Orientally exaggerated colossal figure of his god. In reply I would ask this question: Isn't it obvious today that the truth is the absolute opposite of that statement? *The more God is banished from life the more forlorn and worthless man becomes,* the more he becomes merely a game beast to be hunted and killed. And I venture further to ask: Where in the world does man have any higher dignity than here— where the Son of God discovers human nobility deep beneath the surface of depravity and vice, finds it even in the possessed, the insane, the tainted and infected, and gives his life for them? Isn't it true that every beaten and oppressed man, borne down by anxiety or guilt or inferiority feelings, begins to lift up his head and take a new lease on life when he comes in touch with Jesus of Nazareth. Why? Simply because now all of a sudden he knows: Here is one who treats me as his *brother.* Here is one who sees in me, not only a sinner, a hopeless case, a bundle of nerves, a burden to others, but rather an erring child, but nevertheless a *child* and nothing less than the child of the *Father,* whom he wants to save by the sacrifice of his life and bring back home to the Father's house. I ask you: Where in all the world has anybody ever devised a conception of human nobility or in his boldest moments even dreamed of an ideal image that can equal the dignity which man acquires in the eyes of Jesus? I find it impossible to be afraid to say: Rather a worm in the eyes of Jesus than a god in the eyes of men!

That's why it is the eyes of Jesus Christ that hold the world together, for they give us men a totally new relationship to one another. From this, however, it follows quite simply that now we must put ourselves beneath these eyes. And therefore it is not enough to say: One must keep the commandments and make them the constitutional law of the world. This is very easy to say, but it is not only hard but absolutely impossible to do. One *cannot* "love" someone simply at command or forgive him or have respect for the life and property of another (to name only a few of the things that are mentioned in the commandments) simply because one is commanded to do so. I can do all this only if I stand in the discipleship of this Lord and see the world, my country, my neighbor through his eyes. Seeing them as he sees them makes them look totally different, and this way of "seeing" also gives to *my* conduct and my whole way of living a totally new stamp and an undreamed-of incentive.

Again I say, we should not look out the window at the wicked Babylon and say: Yes, if only our people would find their way back . . . ! We have no cause to beckon like Pharisees and tell them to come to us!

What is happening "outside" is nothing but the macrocosmic reflection of the hate, envy, lies, adultery, and murderous impulses in your heart and my heart. That's why God's saving purpose for the world can be reduced to a very simple formula: *Through the human heart the creation was corrupted and therefore the cure must also begin in man's heart.* This and nothing else is also the very simple reason why the gospel is so often criticized because it appears to have no prescription for a new world order—a prescription, for example, which would provide valid principles for a political platform or the reconstruction of jurisprudence or the social structure. All parties, groups, associations, and governments which attempt to cure the world on this basis and serve up one program, conference, or commission after another must fail, because their thinking does not begin with the light of eternity. Therefore their reforms begin at the wrong place because, paradoxically, they put the cart before the horse.

I say that the gospel contains no prescription for a valid world order but is rather a medicine for our hearts. Right here, at the place where all the sufferings of the world begin, the starting point of that terrible cosmic rupture which today is causing the ground to shake beneath us all, is where Jesus begins with his healing. The painful abscesses which today are breaking out over the whole body of mankind cannot be cured by physicking and lancing them from the outside, but only by cleansing the blood from the inside and renewing the heart, the animating and regulating center of the body. To this heart and center of the world Jesus directs our attention when he teaches us to pray: "Forgive us our debts." What he means is the most secret fatality of the whole world, the inexorable law of the Corsican blood feud and its cognates. He means the contention and strife in countless homes and families. He means the angry, tangled skein of nations, doggedly and savagely throttling and mauling each other in this last year of the great war. And finally, he also means the thunder of hate which will follow this bolt of international strife and which will only gradually die away.

All this Jesus means in this great global prayer, this prayer that truly spans the world.

But he means it all in such a way that he aims it at your

heart and mine; he binds up the salvation and the judgment of the world with the utterly personal relationship which you and I should have with him. When he teaches us to say, "Forgive us our debts," he is saying, "Thou art the man!" But this time he is saying it, not in judgment, but in the sense that "I" and "my heart" should be the place where the new world begins.

The world, my friends, lives by the few righteous in Sodom and Gomorrah; it lives by the few grains of salt which you and I are called to be. The globe itself lives and is upheld as by Atlas arms through the prayers of those whose love has not grown cold. *The world lives by these uplifted hands, and by nothing else!*

So this great prayer of redemption, "Forgive us our debts," causes us to open up our innermost hearts and commit to the gracious hands of God every dreadful thing within them. But when it does that it also bursts open the doors to the innermost chambers and secrets of our whole world and makes us pray vicariously the petition for everybody and everything: "Forgive us our debts."

Dear friends, what becomes more and more important in the message, which I believe I have learned from the Scriptures and which I proclaim as a preacher, is that we must realize the great *world context* in which everything we Christians believe and pray stands. For me everything depends upon our not cultivating a merely private, personal piety, but rather that every time we pray there should come over us the profound and awful consciousness that we are interceding before God for all nations and their ignorant governments, that God has committed to the little company of his church the destiny of the *world,* and that for its sake, and therefore for your sake and my sake, he continues to postpone the last day and the great final reckoning with the world. Again and again we should be awed and thrilled by the immensity of what is entrusted to our fidelity in faith and prayer, awed by what it means that we as Christians should walk as sober men in a drunken world and as freedmen and royal heirs in a world of catastrophe and slavery. Then there will come upon us the holy passion of those whose life it is to determine destiny, to bear and to change the fate of the world by their prayers.

Now what about this forgiveness of debt with which we are to begin with ourselves?

What is forgiveness?

At all events it cannot mean that we cover up a fault with the "mantle of charity." Divine things are never a matter of illusions and deception. On the contrary, before the sin is forgiven the mantle with which it is covered must be removed. The sin must be unmercifully—yes, unmercifully—exposed to the light of God's countenance (Psalm 90). In other words, it must be recognized and acknowledged. Everything that God does is crystal clear and lucid. It never occurs in dim mystical twilight or the semiconsciousness of ecstasy, but in light and in very realistic soberness.

But just because sin is forgiven in all the drastic openness to which it must submit, it is clear from the outset that forgiveness is not a psychological trick like the clever manipulation of a mantle, but that it is a *miracle,* and that therefore one should never mention the words "forgive" and "forget" in the same breath.

What happens in this "miracle" of forgiveness? Everyone of us who can say, "I am a pardoned sinner," knows very well that this can never mean: I do not sin any more; I am holy, or better, though somewhat crassly, I have been cleansed by moral chemistry. No, we know only too well the things that still lurk in our hearts; we know that the wolves still go on howling in the cellars of our life.

Forgiveness therefore cannot mean to be chemically cleansed. It means rather that my sin no longer separates me from God, that it can no longer be a chasm that cuts me off from the Father.

It is exactly what happens when a mother forgives her child or a wife forgives her husband a lie. When a child lies or a husband deceives his wife, something between them is broken. And we say quite correctly: There is something "between" them. And when the mother, the wife forgives, this does not mean: I "forget" it. (She can never forget it. Even in old age she may feel an icy chill when she thinks of that lie which her husband or child uttered long ago.) Forgiveness means: This shall not separate us. The bond of love is stronger than the separating power that would come between.

But how is this possible? Can one seriously say such a thing, especially about God?

By teaching us this petition Jesus points to himself. He is really saying: Because of me, because I am here, this is possible. The Letter to the Hebrews declares that Christ was not ashamed to call us his brethren (2:11), and the reason why he was not ashamed to do so was that he did not look upon us the way we are but at our origin and what we were meant to be. He looked to the fact that once we came from the hands of God and that we should be his royal children. *That's* what he looked at, and therefore he, in whom this origin was preserved in purity and in whom all that God intended for us was present in perfection, was not ashamed to become one of us and share the lot of those who live in darkness and the shadow of death, bound by the chains of guilt and the toils of fear.

For the sake of this one Man, who is our brother and who paid for this brotherhood with his blood, God will forgive us. To this one Man will God look when Jesus takes us by the hand and leads us to the Father's throne. In this one Man he will see all that was committed to our hands, but which we frittered away. In this one Man he will recognize us as his children.

By becoming our brother Jesus Christ ascribes to us everything we once possessed but squandered away, just as in an earthly family a prodigal son can regain respect and dignity by the fact that his respected brother accepts him, takes his part, gives him his confidence, and then proceeds to take upon himself all the hardship that this gift of brotherhood involves and thus allows him to share his own privileges.

Don't you see, that's why the only way I can pray this petition, "Forgive us our debts" is to look to this my royal brother, who holds inviolate in his hand the patent of nobility, the patent on which my name too is written? I can say it only as I rejoice and sing what any child can understand but no man can finish learning:

> Jesus, thy Blood and righteousness
> My beauty are, my glorious dress;
> 'Midst flaming worlds, in these arrayed,
> With joy shall I lift up my head.

The Father comes to meet me and clasps me to his breast because I come with my brother Jesus Christ, wearing the wedding garment that proves my royal lineage. Jesus' cross falls like a bridge across the chasm. *To walk across that bridge —that's what it means to be in the state of forgiveness!*

Then there is one last point in this petition that must be noted, and that is that it immediately becomes practical. In the Christian faith nothing remains shut up in the ghetto of our inner life. Everything in it immediately thrusts out and seeks to become an action. At the next moment God always puts us to work.

In other words, what we ourselves have experienced in forgiveness immediately demands to become effective in our relationship to our neighbor. When God is generous and forgives us ten thousand talents we cannot be petty unforgiving servants and raise a fuss about a few dollars our neighbor owes us (Matthew 18:21 ff.). When God forgives us for hitting him with a club we should manage to put up with the pinpricks we get from our fellows, our neighbor, our boss, our subordinates. For this is actually the ratio between what God forgives us and what we have to forgive our brother.

This is the one and only way to solve the question of guilt that stands between us and our neighbor, the guilt in our marriage, our office, or the queue at the ticket window where somebody shamelessly tries to push us out of line. Only the thought of what God has done for us and what he has forgiven us can suddenly lift us above the situation, can deliver us from the lurking reaction of anger and bitterness and give us the royal freedom to forgive. I say: only this can effect this freedom. In other words, if I myself am not a pardoned sinner, living by the grace of forgiveness, I cannot forgive. Then I can only suppress and control my anger. But this only leads to the storing up of more bitterness and spite, until one fine day it is vented in a sudden explosion. And this happens for the very simple reason that this repression is not based on genuine freedom because it does not spring from a genuine state of redemption and therefore of relaxedness; it was forced and therefore morbid. I can forgive only in the royal freedom of the child of God, as one who himself has been made free and therefore meets others in freedom.

And that brings us back to our starting point: forgiveness provides the sole possibility of the world's ever escaping the law of the echo, that dreadful, chaotic law by which nations and individuals are constantly inflaming and provoking one another because of the "other's fault," and swelling the avalanche of guilt and retribution to ever more gigantic proportions.

We are always echoes. The only question is: echoes of what? Either we are echoes of the injustice, the intrigue, the chicanery, the meanness that is around us, and then we ourselves become scheming, cheating, and mean. Or we are echoes of Jesus Christ and therefore echoes of that forgiving, renewing, creative love that comes to us from the Father. Then we ourselves become loving, renewing, forgiving, creative, and positive.

This is the sole possibility that that endless screw, which we spoke of at the beginning, may ever come to an end and the dreadful law of retaliation be broken.

Jesus Christ gives us a new beginning!

The "old"—which means this blood of ours that keeps crying for retaliation and is capable of becoming a self-destroying lust of "an eye for an eye and a tooth for a tooth"—this "old has passed away, behold, the new has come."

Wherever Jesus Christ is permitted to enter, new life begins, and the new age springs up from the dungeons of the ancient gods of vengeance wherever men bow before the throne of the Father and tongues confess that Jesus Christ is Lord.

Whenever Jesus Christ is accepted as Lord, men have the chance to make a new beginning in their life, and they face possibilities that no world could ever offer of itself.

"Truly this man was a son of God!" (Mark 15:39).

IX

Lead Us Not into Temptation

No temptation has overtaken you that is not common to man. God is faithful, and he will not let you be tempted beyond your strength, but with the temptation will also provide the way of escape, that you may be able to endure it.

I CORINTHIANS 10:13

We are all familiar with the watchword coined by Nietzsche and flung at us by thousands of newspapers and speeches: "Live dangerously."

That motto is a protest against all the snug, respectable Philistinism which is content to go on sliding over safe tracks with as little risk as possible and preferably with a secure pension ahead.

But it has in it another meaning, namely, the inner attitude of the man who has thrown overboard every higher law and

---

* This sermon was the first to be delivered after the Allied occupation of Stuttgart.

authority and taken the helm in his own hands, nay more, the inner attitude of the man who has even pushed aside the hand of God, in which he might be safe, and gone off on his own. For he doesn't want to be "safe"; he wants to live "dangerously."

This man also had to repudiate forgiveness and try to kick down the Cross of the Lord, for what he wants is to be answerable for his own faults and accept all the consequences here and hereafter. Indeed, he yearns to accept even the hazard of eternity. And the Last Judgment will be the last great adventure he proposes to achieve.

Thousands of times we have looked into the faces of these scornful despisers. All of them wanted and want—for we shall always have them—to be the heroic adventurers of life, who have no need for all this stuff. They were and are enamored of "dangerous" living. They exult in being the great poker players of life and taking the risks of climbing to bold heights and descending to the lowest depths.

The experiment turned out to be more miserable than we all thought possible. We pictured the fall of the heroes more heroically. This is no mere "historical" or "political" statement which has no place in church. I mention it only because it may prompt us to ask a decisive question which goes far beyond the moment: May not the cause of this frightful and yet miserable collapse lie in the fact that this talk of "dangerous living" was only a phrase, pure claptrap, in the sense that the real dangers of life were not seen at all, that it was possible, for example, for people to think that the only dangers consist in what a nation assumes in its military struggle and what it risks (historically and biologically) in its gigantic attempt "to gain the whole world"?

And all the while the truth is totally different. The *one and only* danger was, and always will be, that it might "lose its own soul":

that its men, for example, could think that they themselves were making history, and actually did make it—this was one of the losses the nation's soul sustained—whereas they are only blind horses led of God;

that this people should consider itself a chosen people, whereas the fist of God is already raised to dash it to the ground;

that in its temporal tasks it should disregard the Eternal and in its faith in itself fail to see its guilt and need for forgiveness;

that it should imagine that it believes in God, whereas it is the victim of the wiles of the devil and his shimmering soap bubbles;

that it should proceed with fanatical energy to solve economic, social, and political problems and in solving these problems overlook or simply ignore the fact that first and foremost it needs a Redeemer, who would set straight the deepest basis of its personal life, that basis which is the only one upon which we can act.

I ask, are not the real dangers of life right *here*—those dangers of which our nation was utterly unaware and on which it was so hideously shipwrecked—shipwrecked in the very years and moments when it thought it could play the game of "dangerous living" and carpenter together a world view, which, with all its ridiculous affirmation of life and its befuddlement with "strength through joy," blinked the real and the most terrible danger: the danger that there is such a thing as a devil who can lead a man about by the nose in the midst of all his idealism, and—that there is a God, upon whom we can wreck ourselves, because he will not be mocked.

Can one understand at all the tremendous catastrophe that has now befallen us unless it be from this biblical point of view?

Who could be so deluded as to think that this terrible collapse was caused by the dwindling of our power potential or by the superior strength of the enemy or similar factors? All this is true, of course, but they are only the external manifestations of a far more basic fact, that we did not calculate the factor which is "God" in our plans and therefore fell victims to megalomania;

that we violated the commandments of God and therefore got tangled in the towrope of our own unpredictable and brutal instincts;

that we ignored that monumental call, "I am the Lord your God, you shall have no other gods before me," and hence were landed in a giddy ecstasy of power worship which brought the whole world into the field against us;

that we ceased to trust ourselves to the miracle of God's guidance and therefore put our faith in miracle weapons that never came;

that we no longer knew that God is in heaven and man is on earth and therefore could not help but lose all sense of the real proportions of life and consequently were also stricken with blindness in the purely external spheres of political and military relationships.

Is it necessary to go on? These examples should be sufficient to make two things clear to us.

First, that the denial of God and the casting down of the Cross is never a merely private decision that concerns only my own inner life and my personal salvation, but that this denial immediately brings with it the most brutal consequences for the whole of historical life and especially for our own people. "God is not mocked." This is not merely the often cheaply presented theme of pious tracts on individual conversions; no, the history of the world can tell us terrible tales based on that text.

Second, that the questions that have to do with God and the demons have a degree of reality that far surpasses that of external historical factors, whether they be social, economic, or military. The invisible is mightier and also more creative and destructive in history than the visible. Anybody who still has not grasped that our nation with its program of "dangerous living" was wrecked *precisely on this dangerous rock called "God" and nothing else* has no eyes to see. He no longer sees the forest for the trees, and because he sees only individual catastrophes he no longer sees the basic, cardinal catastrophe which is behind them all.

It is fearfully easy to say, "I want to live dangerously" when one has lost one's sense of the real dangers. It is dreadfully easy to say, "I must march bravely and without fear through the dark forest of life and I must not be afraid of the dark," when one has no idea that this forest of life is filled with the armed knights of a very dangerous God who is not mocked.

And here we encounter the real, the biblical, meaning of "living dangerously," which is much deeper than and totally different from what the great adventurers of life imagine.

The petition "Lead us not into temptation" really does show us that life is dangerous, that it is something that can trip us up and ruin us, a place where we can stake everything on the wrong card.

In one of his expositions of this petition, Luther once said, "We are beset before and behind by temptations and cannot throw them off." Luther, we know, saw the world filled with devils who were clutching at him, and in his drastic way he even threw his inkwell at them. Now perhaps we may wag our heads over such a view of life and say: What a poor medieval fool! After all, our modern, enlightened world has emancipated us from this superstitious, specter-haunted twilight. Or do the words stick in our throats, because in this apocalyptic hour we are beginning to understand what Luther saw and what we have forgotten how to see? Just because we do not see a thing or have forgotten how to see it does not mean that it no longer exists.

So beset is life by perils and so great is the danger that we shall be torn away from God and fall into the hands of the false gods!

For this is exactly what temptation means: to allow oneself to be torn away from God. And here again we must not think in terms of peccadilloes and "puppy-sins"; we must not equate temptation with a child's urge to "snitch" candy or our temptation to stay in bed or to show up late for work.

No, temptation has to do with something totally different. It is actually the fact that through small and great events in our life, little fondnesses and great passions, we can be brought to the point where we lose contact with the Father. For there is one thing we must understand clearly (I have spoken of this before) and that is that we hardly ever sever our relationship to God standing up and shaking our fist at heaven like Prometheus, denying and renouncing God with a planned defiance. As a rule this decision against God is made in a far more tepid way; it occurs almost unnoticed by the apostate mind.

For example, I believe that the simple fact of the radio, the movies, and other factors in our modern life have had far more influence upon the decision against God than anti-Christian ideologies and misguided philosophies. Not because the radio and the movies set people against God, but rather because both of them take up so much of our lives that we no longer have opportunity to ask the question of eternity or listen to its question to us. Our whole way of life, including the overburden of work and including the weekend trips we used to take, which took people away from any kind of worship, has had far more to do with the dying away of our relationship with the Father than all the ideological programs. This is the tepid, almost unconscious way of deciding against God. Our way of life must therefore be examined and controlled in the name of eternity.

But the great and noble things, too, can get between the child and the Father. A student who was making the first hesitant attempts to find his way back to Christ once wrote to me when he was ardently at work on a study of Hölderlin:

> For the moment I have no use for the question of Christ, the forgiveness of sins, and all the rest of it. At present my life is completely absorbed with a great passion to discover

Hölderlin for myself that I forget completely what seemed
so important to me not long ago when I felt empty, ex-
hausted, and unoccupied and thought I had to come to
terms with my sin and my despair over the meaning of life.
Now that I am filled to the brim with this great task all
this is quite gone. It seems like a far-away specter, whereas
before it had flesh and blood and attacked me with threats
and demands.

Here again a secret decision is being made, without this
student's being aware of it. It really is true that even the
great things can get between the child and the Father.

So we can rephrase this petition, "Lead us not into temptation," and also say, "Let nothing become a temptation to me."
For everything (mind you, everything!) can become a temptation to me: not only particular urges and addictions which I
may submit to and which prompt me adroitly to put a damper
on God's demanding Word or, even more adroitly, to declare
it irrelevant (why should God have anything to say about my
vaulting ambition or my sexual desires?), but also the great
things in life can become a temptation to me.

What is it, for example, that appears in Luther's hymn "A
Mighty Fortress is our God" as the most dangerous competitor
of the kingdom of God? Not primarily the sexual urge or envy
or hatred or some other vice, but rather the greatest things,
the things most loved in our life: "goods, fame, child, and
wife." In other words, the possessions we may lose (or the fear
of poverty and dependence); the loss of reputation (or the
fear of ostracism and public disapproval); the destitute wife
and the hungry child (or the fear that something may happen
to those we most love on earth); these are the real competitors.

Have not all of these things, the greatest and most beloved
things, often kept people, kept you and me (perhaps especially in the years that lie immediately behind us), from giving our whole loyalty to God, kept us from standing up and
leaving a meeting because Christ was being maligned, kept us

from going to the Party office and saying, "Do with me what you will, but don't dare to lay hands on the soul of my child"? I ask you, has not this great thing, our "fame" in the eyes of men, kept us from forgoing a promotion or standing up for someone who has been humiliated and defamed? These greatest and most loved things, "goods, fame, child, and wife," the very things which I did not want to jeopardize—have I not again and again allowed these things to became a temptation, put them higher than the Kingdom which must remain? Have we not manfully fought the inferior urges within us—people quite rightly took us to be persons whose private life was unimpeachable—and yet, paradoxically, through the greatest and most cherished treasures of our hearts, we have come perilously close to the demons, and day by day we sense that the nearness of God has fled from our lives?

That's how dangerous life is, my friends! For these decisions are by no means trifles. The dangerousness of life lies precisely in the fact that the dangers lurk in unexpected places and that the wildest wolves that lie in wait for us always wear the most harmless-looking sheep's clothing, that they may even hide themselves behind the faces of the persons we most love.

It is precisely the positive and great things in our life that need to be taken in hand. Jesus did not say, "It is impossible for a *harlot* to enter the kingdom of heaven." He did say, "How hard, indeed, impossible, it is for a *rich man* to enter the kingdom of God." And these rich men are not all crude hucksters; they may be people of culture and an ordered way of life, with rich and broad minds, elevated and yet imperiled by all the treasures of culture and education.

The tempter in the wilderness, of whom we shall have more to say in the next sermon, made nothing but grand and captivating proposals to Jesus. He did not forget to appeal to his idealism, to his piety, and even the Word of God. He suggested to him the fantastic idea of controlling all humanity by offering him all the kingdoms of this world; and still there was only one thing he wanted, and that was to separate him from the Father, with the help of these grand ideas which might well intoxicate a human mind.

This is the first surprise we encounter when we begin to think about temptation.

The record is this. When we succumb to the temptation to do something without God, this may result at first in great success. The worship of success is generally *the* form of idol worship which the devil cultivates most assiduously. Here is where even the most serious men may have a weak spot. The time that lies immediately behind us provides abundant material to illustrate this. We could observe in the first years after 1933 the almost suggestive compulsion that emanates from great successes and how, under the influence of these successes, men, even Christians, stopped asking in whose name and at what price they were achieved. Because success is the greatest narcotic of all, the devil, the false prophets (Matthew 24:24), the beast from the depths of the earth (Revelation 13:13) perform great wonders.

I say, it is quite possible that at first we may have great success when we succumb to the temptation to live our life without God. Perhaps the best example of this is provided by the phenomenon which we call "fanaticism." The challenge to live and fight "fanatically" means, after all, to live and fight in such a way that a man no longer sees anything but his goal, that he refuses to entertain the slightest questioning of his struggle, and that therefore he must also refuse to face the question whether this struggle and this goal are "good" or "bad." For the question of good or bad is something that could immediately upset my enthusiasm and fill me with scruples and misgivings, which might be detrimental to my fanatical singlemindednes. It is quite clear to us from our own experience that at first this fanatical devotion produces great success and that because of its lack of inhibitions and scruples it possesses an almost incomparable historical potency. But as Christians we know that being "under God" is the sole guarantee for the continuance of the world and that when we do not lay claim to this guarantee the chaos of his vengeance intervenes. The tempter not only leads men away from God, but after a brief interval of prosperity, he leads them to the abyss. And here again the last book of the Bible says the conclusive thing: the devil must work feverishly because "he knows that his time is short" and that the short-term loans he hands out will very soon be called in by God.

Now we understand a little of what "dangerous living" really means. We are beset on every side and tempted by the big *and* the little things in our life; we are tempted equally by our passions *and* our ideals. There is nothing the tempter does not know how to use in order to tear nations and individuals from God's hand. Outside and inside our hearts, high above our heads, where ideals dwell, and down in the cellars where the wild wolves of the senses play havoc, everywhere dwell the tempting powers.

That's why life is dangerous. And God teaches us through his Word to recognize these dangers because the greatness of a danger always increases when it is hidden and unknown. Because God knows this about our life, the Letter to the Ephesians speaks of faith in terms of weapons and armor and describes the life of the disciple as a soldier's existence. His life is a struggle against mortal dangers and deadly temptations.

In this respect too, Jesus brought us not peace but a sword. In this respect too, he sends us out as sheep in the midst of wolves.

It was in this same knowledge that Albrecht Dürer created the famous engraving, "Knight, Death and the Devil." For all the tempting powers are there in that picture: not only the toads and salamanders, the symbols of the base powers and instincts that would drag him down; not only the specter of death that would strike terror into him and undermine his faith with its dread; but also the homelike castle in the background, the embodiment of "goods, fame, child, and wife," of all that is loved and dear and familiar, which he must forgo. For even this most beloved is a danger to him, now that he is ordained to battle, a great danger, if it should entice him to its peace at the wrong moment and tempt him to rest and rejoice when he should be fighting the battle.

And here we come to the decisive question of how to cope with this dangerous, seductive life, of how we can attain to that "blessed man," of whom the Letter of James speaks, who endures trial and receives "the crown of life."

In the first place it is important when we face this question to give heed to the message that is found in Jesus' high-priestly prayer: "I do not pray, O Father, that thou shouldst take them out of the world, but that thou shouldst keep them from evil" (John 17:15). In other words, we shall *remain* in a state of siege and we shall never be free from the dangers of life. Rather Jesus teaches his own to pray, "Let nothing become a temptation to us," and thus makes it clear that *everything* can become a temptation, indeed, that life itself is but one long peril and temptation.

He does not spare us suffering, but he is on our side. He does not free us from the burdens of life, but he helps us carry them. He does not simply banish death; he permits the last enemy to remain; but he helps us in our death, and though we must depart, he never departs from us. He does not spare us the valleys of the shadow, but he goes through them with us, always a shepherd who leads us and a rod and staff that will not let us stumble.

And so he deals with *temptations* too. He does not allow us to emigrate to the islands of the blessed where there is no temptation, but he helps us in the midst of this world which is beset by deadly and devilish footpads waiting to waylay us at every step.

How does he do this?

Well, just as Jesus, by becoming man, comes right down to the front-line trenches and fights with us against the hostile powers of death and suffering and sin, so he also draws us into his own life. He not only stands beside *us,* but *we* also stand beside *him.*

And where does he stand? He stands *in the wilderness alone,* and the tempter has fled, but the angels are ministering to him. He stands in *hell*—"he descended into hell"— and he has won the victory over Satan and all his demonic spirits. He stands at the *right hand of God* in kingly sovereignty; and because he stands there, even the satanic powers, the great adversaries and antichrists must serve him, and against their will become the functionaries of his gracious plans.

Where does that leave the tempter? Now he must obey a regime which he himself does not understand. What does the devil accomplish except to drive Job straight into the arms of the very God from whom he was trying to separate him? What can Nero and his modern counterparts do? They too, instead of destroying the church, accomplish nothing except to compel it to achieve an ultimate maturity in the refining furnace of suffering. (Don't we all sense this today? Has not the church of Jesus Christ become different and more mature in these years of persecution? Have not the talents entrusted to us increased so much, despite all the unfaithfulness in these years, that we must tremble lest we bury them again and let them go to the dogs?) The fact that we stand beside Jesus means that now the tempter can only bark but not bite, that the serpent's tail may rattle but his head is already crushed (Genesis 3:15). He has been so stripped of his power that he can no longer separate us from the love of God which is in Christ Jesus our Lord. Nothing can separate us from his fellowship so long as we hold on to his hand.

His hand!

Here we must understand that Jesus is teaching us something about the tempter by telling us to *pray* against him. In other words, we cannot "act" against him. How should we be able to stand him off with the strength of our own soul and will when he has already built a bridge-head in this soul? We have every reason to distrust the broken-down and undependable fighting power of our own soul. This ought to be clear from Jesus' controversy with the Pharisees. For, after all, the Pharisees had undertaken a tremendous, systematic attempt, which was thought out to the smallest detail, to make themselves acceptable to God through their ethical conduct and thus to combat the power of evil. But as they worked at it, it turned out to be something totally different. It became an attempt to cultivate by means of moral struggle an ultimate, subtle, scarcely visible egoism that made claims upon God by pointing to its good works. Thus it did the very thing the devil wants to accomplish, namely, to drive us out of the child-relationship and force us into the role of competitors of God with all the presumption and arrogant defiance which that involves.

The point is that we are not contending against flesh and blood—that would be simple!—but rather against "principalities and powers and the spiritual hosts of wickedness in heavenly places" (Ephesians 6:12). And there every human arm cannot but fail.

Therefore Jesus directs us to resort to *prayer* when we meet the tempter, and thus shows us that contact with the Father is the chief means by which to challenge the tempter. Only the Father's hand, which we hold on to, can ward off the devil's onslaught. We ourselves are far too ramshackle not to provide the tempter with opportunities to slip through the back door of our heart while we look straight ahead and march out to do brave battle with our well-meant ethos and our honest idealism.

So long as we stand within our Lord's field of power, no power can touch us. Nobody and nothing can break the bond of faith which the Lord has established with his own. He has promised to be with us in temptation, and even those who fall he pursues and raises up again.

So here again Jesus is completely positive. The knight makes no to-do whatsoever about fighting death and the devil; he does not raise his weapons against the fiends that beset his path. If he were to get into a skirmish with every tramp, every desire and appetite, every "dirty dog" that growls within him, he would soon be involved in such a scuffle that he would be stopped in his tracks. Instead he rides straight on and refuses to allow the tempting powers to dictate his course of action. In the distance he sees his Lord, beckoning in encouragement and preparing to receive him. As long as he keeps his eyes on *him* the vermin on his path cannot upset him.

This is the positive element in the Christian life: We do not squabble with the demonic powers; we look to our Lord. *He does all the rest.* Then, mysteriously, everything that would overpower us is banished.

Here is a simple little experience that will serve as an illustration. I heard of a young man, filled with the exuberance of life and passion, who therefore had great difficulty contending with the temptations of the body. He fought a brave battle against them and struggled manfully against the lurid images of his imagination. He suppressed his urges because he wanted to remain clean, and he also *prayed.* But just because he was so preoccupied with it, even though he was fighting against it, he became more and more involved, and the inevitable result was that time and again he succumbed. But he was a Christian and one day he stopped praying, "Lord, help me to fight temptation, help me to conquer my desires," and ventured to say, "Lord, I thank thee for this great gift of thy creation which thou hast given to me. Help me to use it to thine honor"—and suddenly the spell was broken.

This shows us how positive Jesus wants us to be. There is a sense in which we can say that we should not fight against temptation, since this only mires us more deeply. We should rather keep our eyes on the Lord, like the knight riding past death and the devil; we should "look to Jesus the pioneer and perfecter of our faith"; then we shall ride through our temptations—"like those who dream" (Psalm 126:1), like victors. He who looks to the King, he who does this enormously "positive" thing, to him all the rest, including the overcoming of temptation, will be "added."

We can never put too much trust in Jesus and we can never put too little trust in ourselves.

So when we pray, "Lead us not into temptation," we should remember that it is Jesus himself who is teaching us to pray this petition and is therefore assuming the responsibility that this prayer will be heard. It is amazing how he helps those who really venture everything—"goods, fame, child, and wife"—upon him. You can ask them yourself—and there are not a few who have done this in these last years. Not one of them was disappointed. God never lets a man down.

He hears the petition, but something far more than mere hearing happens: he also walks beside us as we go through the fire of temptation, "for we have not a high priest who is unable to sympathize with our weaknesses, but one who in every respect has been tempted as we are, yet without sinning" (Hebrews 4:15). He is not only the Lord who hears but also the Brother who bears our burdens with us.

He is the goal toward which we strive *and* the companion on the way.

He is the one who waits for the faithful wayfarer with a crown *and* also the one who accompanies him through all the fires and dark defiles.

What is the meaning and purpose of our life? That we should not lose our way and fail to find him who comes to meet us from the other side—him who is eager to welcome every one of us who comes out of great tribulation and wild temptations, falling often but graciously lifted up again and again, eager to greet us with the Lord's salutation to his faithful servant:

Blessed art thou, the faithful,
For all is well with thee;
Thou bearest with thanksgiving
The crown of victory;
For God himself now places
In thy right hand the palms.
To Him, who bore thy sorrow,
Sing then thy joyful psalms.

PAUL GERHARDT

X

Deliver Us from Evil

Then Jesus was led up by the Spirit into the wilderness to be tempted by the devil.

And he fasted forty days and forty nights, and afterward he was hungry.

And the tempter came and said to him, "If you are the Son of God, command these stones to become loaves of bread."

But he answered, "It is written, 'Man shall not live by bread alone, but by every word that proceeds from the mouth of God.'"

Then the devil took him to the holy city, and set him on the pinnacle of the temple, and said to him, "If you are the Son of God, throw yourself down; for it is written, 'He will give his angels charge of you,' and 'On their hands they will bear you up, lest you strike your foot against a stone.'"

Jesus said to him, "Again it is written, 'You shall not tempt the Lord your God.'"

Again, the devil took him to a very high mountain, and showed him all the kingdoms of the world and the glory of them; and he said to him, "All these I will give you, if you will fall down and worship me."

> *Then Jesus said to him, "Begone, Satan! for it is written, 'You shall worship the Lord your God and him only shall you serve.'"*
>
> *Then the devil left him, and behold, angels came and ministered to him.*

Matthew 4:1–11

Literally translated, this petition reads: "Deliver us from *the evil.*" And here again what is meant is not evil in general, and therefore what is bad, imperfect, vicious, perhaps even demonic, but rather the "evil one." It is therefore a *personal* magnitude. It is nothing less than—the devil. From his tyranny may the Father deliver us. This is what Jesus teaches us to pray.

The petition "Lead us not into temptation" has already pointed in this direction, for in our last study we saw that, behind all the dangers in our life and behind all the dark menaces that overshadow it, there is a dark, mysterious, spellbinding figure at work. Behind the temptations stands *the* tempter, behind the lie stands *the* liar, behind all the dead and the bloodshed stands *the* "murderer from the beginning."

Several decades ago some preachers who had to speak about this figure would probably have begun by apologizing in more or less decent fashion for venturing as a modern and educated person to mention the word "devil" at all. And they probably would have taken some pains to convince their hearers that, after all, the Middle Ages had some very wise ideas in its conception of the devil—though naturally expressed in all too "realistic" terms which were in accord with its time, but which we could no longer share. . . . The preacher would perhaps have continued: We today must take these crude images of medieval fantasy (the fact that there really is a personal devil) and recast them in the crucible of our modern, informed understanding and distill them in all kinds of philosophical retorts until we had transformed this green-eyed devil with the cloven hoof and the smell of brimstone into a properly spiritualized "concept of evil" which we might expect modern man to accept.

Dear friends, in our time we have had far too much contact with demonic powers;

we have sensed and seen how men and whole movements have been corrupted and controlled by mysterious, abysmal powers, leading them where they had no intention of going;

we have observed all too often how an alien spirit can ride people and change the very substance of men who before may have been quite decent and reasonable persons, driving them to brutalities, delusions of power, and fits of madness of which they never appeared to be capable before;

year by year we have seen an increasingly poisonous atmosphere settling down upon our globe and we sense how real and almost tangible are the evil spirits in the air, seeing an invisible hand passing an invisible cup of poison from nation to nation and throwing them into confusion;

I say that we have seen all this too clearly; we have been far too shocked by all this for me to have to prepare your mind and mine in order to discuss the question of the devil without embarrassing you. The overwhelming power of these experiences is so strong that it simply breaks through all the intellectual insulation which we are so prone to interpose in order to keep out these dark powers.

So we shall leave undecided the question whether there is a devil, and rather ask what the Bible says about him, and then compare his biblical portrait with what we encounter in our apocalyptic times. Perhaps it is not at all difficult to show that both images are the same.

Why, actually, is the tempter so dangerous? For if he were not so dangerous, then surely Jesus would not have taught us to pray for deliverance from him. Then presumably he himself would not have been obliged to march out against him and spend his whole earthly life fighting this invisible enemy. I would answer this question of why the demonic power is so dangerous simply by saying that it is because he cannot be recognized, simply because he does not have the characteristic hoofs by which one could recognize him. If he had a passport, under the heading "Special Characteristics" there would be written "None." The devil is a master of disguise, and one important specialty of his tactics consists in his hiding behind positive values and ideals.

This can be illustrated by means of a simple, everyday example. When a seducer tries to bring another person into his power, he certainly does not begin by saying, "Come, I'll teach you something evil; I'll show you a sin." If he were to begin his seduction in such a foolish way, our conscience would doubtless be shocked and we would seek to escape the temptation.

But the tempter would never begin in such a stupid way. He always tries to represent his offer as something that will lead to positive and significant goals. So he says, "Come, I will teach you something interesting, something pleasurable, something that will give you a glorious thrill and give you the chance to live to the full." The classical example of this technique of temptation is that which was demonstrated in the temptation of Jesus in the wilderness.

And now as we discuss this a bit, and since this will require us to look into some deep abysses, we must right from the beginning hold fast to this tremendously comforting thought: At the most perilous point in our life, namely, the place where we must do battle with the tempter for life or death, there Jesus stood *too*, there he stands *beside* us. His heart *too* was shaken by the grandiose jugglery with which the tempter tried to bemuse him. For, as we have said, what the tempter does always has stature. It never lacks grand perspectives and the touch of idealism. But he who has the Lord beside him, that Lord who was "tempted as we are" and stands in the same rank with us, he who has beside him this Lord against whom the tempter's charm could not prevail—that person's faith then begins to operate like a kind of divining-rod by which he is able to "distinguish between spirits" and which reacts immediately whenever the devil appears, no matter how deceiving his mask may be, whether he disguises himself as national idealism, or a democratic order that is going to make the whole world happy, whether he comes with a Bible in his hand or dripping with the oil of pious phrases, or whether he operates with the doctrines of some plausible sounding and seemingly sound philosophy. The Lord who stood in the wilderness never departs from his own when the hour of temptation breaks in upon them.

Jesus is the Victor! He has already won, and all our struggles are only rear-guard battles and mop-up actions, all of which are under the sign of that victory which the Lord achieved for us all in the wilderness.

And yet how positive and appealing are the means with which the tempter operates! To understand this we need only to think of the *third temptation,* in which the devil took Jesus to a very high mountain where all the kingdoms of the world and their glory lay spread out before him: "All these will I give you . . . !"

What a heady, intoxicating prospect that was! For when the devil offered him the kingdoms of the world he was by no means appealing only to the baser instincts, the vile thirst to satisfy the ambition to secure one zone of influence after another, or the brutal urge to power that hankers for dominion. No, when he made this offer he was appealing, as it were, to Jesus' "idealism" and the highest aspirations of his soul; for if Jesus were elevated to the sovereignty of the world, this would seem to give him the opportunity to use his power to the glory of God and carry on the mighty work of "Christianizing the world." Would not any human heart, even the heart of the Son of God, tremble at the magnitude of this idea? For if this were so, if the whole earth were led to Christianity "with power," then the disciples would no longer need to have the oppressive feeling that they were so defenseless and exposed and that the history of the world was passing them by and paying no heed to them. Then they would cease to be "only" the quiet in the land, ignored by the loud, rushing stream of world events. Then they would no longer face the depressing embarrassment of not being able to prove the existence and power of their Lord when they were asked. Then, when the terrible catastrophes struck and the specter of doubt and despair of God lifted its head, they would no longer need to blush in silence when the godless raised their malicious question: "Where is your God?"

All this would suddenly be changed—if Jesus were the sovereign of the world, if he had the armies and their flags and standards at his disposal. Then even the vilest mockers would be silenced and they would bow down before him. Then his presence would be visible in every edict, in every uniform, in every flag, and, if anybody asked whether he existed and whether he was a mighty sovereign, we would only have to point to all these things.

No missionary would ever again be left defenseless on alien coasts to face the butchers of men, if—yes, if Jesus were the sovereign of the world.

Is not this in fact a great idea, a positively dizzying prospect?

Or we think of the *first temptation,* in which the devil tries to induce the Lord to turn stones into bread. Here Jesus suddenly sees himself confronted with this tremendous possibility: *I* could provide men with bread! I could perform this undreamed of act of brotherly love by feeding the hungry. This in itself must have been an extraordinarily powerful and appealing motive. But when we examine it closer, the charm of this devilish overture becomes still greater. For the implications of providing bread are by no means confined to the body. It involves infinitely more than that. The satisfaction of hunger would immediately entail tremendous intellectual consequences, for do we not have control of men, control of the minds of men when we have control of their bread? As the proverb says: Whose bread I eat, his song I sing! Anybody who wants to rule, and especially anybody who wants to rule the minds of men, must first get control of the bread problem. When people have food and clothing and shelter, they usually "join the parade." Then they get over their conscientious scruples and renounce their old faith with relatively light hearts and find the new gods quite unobjectionable. With a full stomach, people are glad to hand over blanket authority to the bread-provider. There have been many hunger revolts in history, but not many based on conviction. The food question is really one of the keys to world history. All this the tempter intimated to the Lord. And again, isn't this a great idea: If I can bind people to myself and get them to sing my tune by feeding them, why shouldn't I try to bind them to *God* in this way? If with empty stomachs they think it bigoted to sing a chorale, but they are willing to sing for their host after a good supper—well, I'll give them their supper "for *God's* sake" and their stomach's sake.

So it is possible that the right solution of the food problem may have enormous significance for the kingdom of God and its extension.

But the bemusing questions which the tempter keeps trying to drop like sweet poison into the mind of Jesus go even further. Feeling the impact of this satanic insinuation, Jesus must now ask himself: Will not many become unfaithful to me (this is surely what the devil was suggesting) simply because they will be afraid—and quite rightly—that they will lose their jobs and their bread, if they follow me? It may be costly for them to confess me. Many will therefore shun this confession or throw it overboard when the pinch comes. But the moment I give them bread the dilemma will be solved, and suddenly the conflict between God and "goods, fame, child, and wife" will vanish. Then the Christian faith will be popular for there will be no risks involved. I could turn millions of adherents, who simply flinch from me as long as I remain only an invisible and seemingly helpless Lord, into my most faithful followers. Ought I not therefore to give bread for God's sake and the sake of these millions? Ought I not to restrict the risk and the venture that faith demands? Ought I not to make discipleship a rewarding and paying proposition? Otherwise, what will happen to the great masses who are out after bread and circuses? Does not love and compassion demand that I couple the kingdom of God and the breadbasket, and reward my adherents with food?

And again the question arises: Is not this a great idea of the devil, which might be a solution to the deepest conflicts of human life?

And the *second temptation,* that Jesus throw himself down from the pinnacle of the temple—naturally, on the Sabbath when a great crowd would be present to be astonished by the feat—this second temptation too has a seductive grandeur about it. For what it means is that the tempter is challenging the Son of God to indulge in publicity and propaganda. He is suggesting to him something like this:

"Now, Jesus of Nazareth, you are starting out all wrong, if you think you can win people and call them to decision by preaching and ministering and personal encounter. Most people do not have the maturity to deal with such personal questions anyhow.

"Do you have such poor knowledge of people, Jesus of Nazareth, that you insist on riding their consciences? Just look at them: most of them have no wills at all; they are conscienceless copies of the great mass who swim along with the crowd and are pushed around by every wind that blows. They are purely sensual beings, moved not by ideas but by sensations and impressions. Look at any show or night club, Jesus of Nazareth! There they are—all spectators: the fools and the intelligent, the upright and the scoundrels. And all of them gaze entranced at the stage where the artists perform their tricks. Their hearts stop beating when the acrobat makes his mortal leap, and they all break out in one single burst of applause when the trick succeeds and the nervous tension is released. Look at them, Jesus of Nazareth; it's their nerves you have to appeal to, for they all have nerves and they react immediately with their nerves. You should get this straight, Jesus of Nazareth: As far as the great masses are concerned, the conscience is a completely secondary organ. Most people do not live by their conscience at all. They do not live on the basis of responsibility and personal decision. They live by their nerves, their sensations, the herd instinct. If you want to win the world (even if you want to win it *for God*), you will have to satisfy their primitive sensuality, their need to have their nerves titillated. If you can impress them there, they will flock after you, and they will *also* believe what you tell them about the higher things of life. After all, Jesus of Nazareth, what you are telling them is something good (says the devil!). After all, you want to lead them to your Father. Why shouldn't you condition their hearts with this propaganda appeal to their senses? Then they will also be able to take in the higher message you proclaim as a 'redeemer.' "

This idea, too, is not without greatness. It could put Jesus' mission on a totally new and tremendously promising basis.

In short, everything the devil says is enormously positive. These are stupendous goals, staggering in their persuasiveness.

And yet these ideals and grand prospects are nothing but a delusive cloak to cover up—now let us say it—a cloven hoof, to cover up the fact that all this would only serve the devil: "If you will fall down and worship me!"

How so?

In order to understand why this is so, let us think back to the *third temptation,* to the moment when the devil offered the Lord Christ all the kingdoms of the world.

In the thousand years of Christian history that lie behind us we have actually learned something about the chances and temptations which were inherent in this moment. For this millennium, which is now coming to an end, was the Constantinian age of the church. It offered the intoxicating opportunity for Christianity to enter into a secure alliance with the public, above all with the state. One need only think of the motto, "Throne and Altar," to understand this. The schools were almost automatically Christian schools; the press was for the most part at the disposal of the church; the guilds had their reserved places in the sanctuaries. Did not this firm alliance of church and state, of parish and public present a tremendous chance for Christianity to permeate all the areas of life? Was this not an impressive expression of Christ's claim upon the whole of human life?

But now, since 1933, we have seen this "wholesale" Christianity of the great masses and mere "holders of baptismal certificates" simply collapse because it led only to a Christian façade for public life, behind which lingered the gods and myths of a pagan and atheistic age, gods and myths which were only waiting for the moment when they could tear down the façade and proclaim their dominion openly.

And surely they have done this impressively and consistently enough. Can any of us be anything but utterly astonished at the manifestations of paganism and neopaganism that suddenly appeared among our nominally Christian people? Would we ever have thought it possible that, in a country in which almost everybody was baptized and confirmed or at least brought up under Christian influence, hundreds of thousands would gather together in the Berlin Sports Palace and the largest auditoriums in every city and cheer themselves hoarse over the German faith-movement and other pagan ideologies?

Suddenly God led his church out of its accustomed public place in the Constantinian age. He allowed it to be driven into the ghetto of its own church walls and in some instance into the catacombs. And in these narrow places there occurred with God's help a process of maturation which caused the church to find its way back to the substance of its message and its biblical foundations. The very fact that God took from the church its public position was a demonstration of his gracious providence, whereby he separated the wheat from the confusing chaff, cleared the jungle of so-called "Christianity" of everything except the two towering trees of "Scripture and Confession," brought forth the "holy remnant," and sustained his church through it all.

Not that this ghetto is the ideal, not that the church should remain within her walls and renounce the world! I should hope never to be so misunderstood. But it does make a difference whether the world is simply labeled as Christian by higher authorities and surrounded with a Christian façade, thus creating a mere Potemkin village of sham Christianity, or whether a church which has been matured in the ghetto and catacombs, a "holy remnant," tempted and tested in the fires of suffering, emerges from these walls and with authority proclaims Christ's dominion over the world. This was the only interpretation that Jesus put upon the great commission when he commanded the disciples to go out into the world in the name of their Lord to whom all power was given.

The other temptation, namely, the temptation to exercise power by means of bread and control of the sources of food, is perhaps the peril of the church of Jesus today. For, after all, we face the fact that the church is one of the very few trusted factors from the past which survived the great deluge. This fact has its greatness but also its dangers. The church of Jesus and its bishops are now solicited for aid and counsel in many public affairs, even in political matters. The church of Jesus has the opportunity—at least for a brief period—

to exercise power, to make use of the long lever, and by possible joint control of the food supply to bring people into the sphere of its influence.

Woe to it, if it does so! Woe to it, if it seeks to achieve its destiny of leading men to the Cross and bringing them into a living personal relationship with Jesus Christ by employing the instruments of power and the breadbasket! Woe to it, if even in a single case it allows the fact that a person is a member of the church or has left the church to work to his advantage or detriment! Then we would soon have exchanged the red and the brown terror for the black terror. And the black terror would be the worst. For in the other forms of terror only *men* are dishonored, whereas this most dreadful species of tyranny would desecrate the very *Cross* on which the Lord Christ died in helplessness in order to bring the world back home.

Woe to it, if the church of Jesus does not remain beneath this powerless Cross, if it does not speak out openly—no matter what the powers and pressures are that make it neces-sary—and say what is right and what is wrong, at least as clearly as it has sometimes done under past dictators!

Woe to it, if it does not prefer to give up all its influence rather than deny the truth, if it is not prepared to be like a sheep among wolves, no matter what the nationality of these wolves may be! The church has no other mission except to proclaim the commandments of God and to tell the imprisoned that they are free, the blind that they shall see, and the guilty and heavy laden that the Cross of Calvary is there for them. It was not for nothing that God allowed the church of Jesus to suffer for twelve years, and thus brought it to a place of blessing which we dare not now deny.

It is only human, "all too human" that someone who has been in a concentration camp for Jesus' sake or—as in my own case—dismissed, forbidden to travel or to speak, and hampered in every way, should now desire to get back into the stream of things and go ahead at full speed, to have the feeling of "power" which he has been deprived of for so long, in order to make up for the time lost.

I say this is "human, all too human," and we are actually seeing some evidences of this human delight in power within the church. But we must have nothing to do with it. This is not what Jesus Christ died for! The church of Jesus has no business to take revenge or to sit in judgment. The church must be a *mother* to all who are weary and heavy laden, to all who have strayed and gone wrong—even to those who have forsaken their mother in the last decade and fallen victim to strange ideas. And therefore its task is not to look to the great and powerful, to the "Americans" and the "English," but rather to visit the prisoners and preach the gospel to those who cannot help the church because they have no privileges to bestow.

Jesus himself quite consciously passed up the great chances and the great moments for making propaganda in his life. When he had the chance to speak to great crowds, when he might have taken advantage of the wildest ovations of enthusiastic hearers, he made his way through the midst of them and went away to be alone with God or to help a sick person or a burdened conscience. This was precisely the time when he turned to the individual, who was completely lacking in influence and could not make him king. So the church too must bear witness to the truth and the love of God in this unpopular way and turn to those who need its help and comfort. Who was ever more unpopular than its Master? But the servant dare not be above his master.

So Jesus saw through the intoxicating visions and glittering prospects which the devil conjured up before him. He renounced power—even the power that he might have used for his purpose, the Christianization of the world. He knew that the very substance of his message would be altered and falsified if the child were put under the slightest compulsion to go back home to the Father. For then the child would become a slave and the Father a tyrant.

So he rose up from the place where the kingdoms of the world shimmered before him, where crowns flashed and banners rustled, and hosts of enthusiastic people were ready to acclaim him, and quietly walked the way of poverty and suffering to the Cross.

He walked the road where the great and the rich of this world will despise him, but where he is the brother of sinners, the companion of the forsaken and lonely, the sharer of the lot of all who are shelterless and know not where to lay their head, the comrade of the insulted and injured, to whom he reaches down from his shameful Cross.

With all these he associates himself, he who could have possessed the whole world.

And that is why the story closes with the angels ministering to him, which means that the presence of the Father was with him. The angels will always be where he is, even, and most particularly, in the darkest places of his journey through the deep. And in Gethsemane, too, one of them will come to him and strengthen him.

Did he stake his life on the wrong card, this Jesus of Nazareth? Did he make a bad exchange when in the hour of temptation he preferred the presence of the angels and the presence of the Father to the riches of this world? If he had accepted the riches of this world and their "glory" he would be forgotten today. He would have become a great king in history, recorded in the history books of our schools. He would have become a venerated museum piece—*if* he had signed the pact with the devil. But because he suffered and in suffering learned obedience, he has become our brother and our king, and therefore we too know that this is our destiny:

> And he who fain would kiss, embrace
> This little Child with gladness
> Must first endure with him in grace
> The rack of pain and sadness.

We must not only die to the baser powers of temptations, the enchantment and allure of the senses and the wild fever of revenge and ambition—for when we are bewitched by these we cannot hear the "voice"—but we must also be willing to die to the "ideal" motives, to "goods, honor, child, and wife." We must even maintain a certain distance from the great and gladsome, dear and familiar things of this world, as we saw in the picture of the "Knight, Death, and the Devil." And the truth is that this is no small thing. All of it is painful, it is all a "rack of pain and sadness," or at least can become so. But because of it we can embrace Him and know the presence of the angels. God is blessed and because of this blessedness all this is worthwhile. Never will we regret it if we choose the way of the Cross in the hour of temptation, for it is the way of the Master. In every case God is richer than the devil is evil; and none who has ever followed him has ever regretted the "rack of pain and sadness."

May the church of Jesus not dream away the hour to which it has now been called. It faces great promises and terrible temptations. May the church be a mother who bends low to help the lost and defend their cause; and may it not become a courtesan who looks with longing glances at the glory of the mighty.

May it be a comforting beacon, proclaiming to all men that at least in one place in this world of hate and revenge there is love, because, beyond all comprehension, the Son of God died for this world. And if it must preach judgment, if it must call down woe upon the people and interpret the fearful signs of the times, then may it never do so pharisaically, as one who had no share in the great guilt. But rather may it do so as a mother, whose own soul is pierced through by a sword; may it do so as did Jesus Christ himself, who uttered the cry of judgment over Jerusalem in a voice that was choked with tears.

XI

For Thine Is the Kingdom and the Power and the Glory, Forever, Amen.

Being asked by the Pharisees when the kingdom of God was coming, he answered them, "The kingdom of God is not coming with signs to be observed; nor will they say, 'Lo, here it is!' or 'There!' for behold, the kingdom of God is in the midst of you."

And he said to the disciples, "The days are coming when you will desire to see one of the days of the Son of man, and you will not see it. And they will say to you, 'Lo, there!' or 'Lo, here!' Do not go, do not follow them. For as the lightning flashes and lights up the sky from one side to the other, so will the Son of man be in his day."

LUKE 17:20–24

All of us who are living through these, humanly speaking, hopeless times have within us a yearning for a *sign* from God. With troubled hearts we keep looking to see whether somewhere we can find a tangible meaning in which, contrary to all appearances, there will be some evidence that God is really governing the world. We yearn to

146

meet somebody, anybody in whom we may find some trace of the presence of God. We search for any plausible thought that might help to interpret and understand the riddle of this world in the light of eternity. So we all wait for a hopeful sign for the future to assure us that a countenance full of grace and not the stony face of the sphinx hovers over the world.

So we pray the Lord's Prayer to the end, and, because we are speaking to the Father in heaven, we do so in the secret hope that some sign, some reason will appear to prove to us that our prayers are not uttered into a void and that therefore we do not pray in vain for the coming of the kingdom of God, for daily bread, for deliverance from temptation, and for the forgiveness of our sin.

And now all of a sudden at the close of the Lord's Prayer one such decisive reason is given—a reason that gives meaning to all the preceding petitions. Suddenly we come upon the little word "for," which puts a foundation under all that has gone before: "For thine is the kingdom and the power and the glory, forever." Manifestly, what this is saying is this: "Just because this kingdom is in force and because thou art Lord in it, thou hast the power to hear us. Therefore thou art also merciful to give us our daily bread and forgive us our sins."

What we think of as we say these concluding words of the Lord's Prayer is this: God be thanked that now we have this ground to stand upon when we pray. The reason why we can pray as we do is that the kingdom belongs to God and the power and glory too.

But is this reason actually true? Did not Jesus himself say, "My kingdom is not of this world"? And did he not say this at the critical moment of his earthly life, namely, before Pontius Pilate? In the very moment, therefore, when the kingdom of God had every opportunity to prove its divine superiority in competition with the powers of this earth. But if it is necessary at such a moment to emphasize that it "is not of this world," that it simply will not compete with the visible, brutal powers of this world, then how in the world are we going to see it at all?

Doesn't this mean that the whole thing dissolves into nothingness again, leaving the Lord's Prayer hanging in the air?

If this kingdom is so little of this world that nobody could be found at the judgment of Pilate to spring to the defense of their Lord—with the worldly, all too worldly means of power—then, we may say, there will be no bread in this kingdom either, no sound basis for material existence, no secure defense. Once when I was speaking to a Christian farmer whose daughter had been assaulted in his presence, I thought I saw in his eyes for a moment this dreadful doubt that he and his family, who wanted to be members of this kingdom of God, were nevertheless left defenseless and exposed to the terrible powers of the world at the critical moment.

So again we ask ourselves, doesn't it all turn out to be a vague, unpredictable, unverifiable matter of the future?

And when we ask this depressing question we are in exactly the same place as the men of the Bible. It is not at all as if we in the twentieth century were the first to be harried and worried by this question. No, the people who were with Jesus himself were tormented by it.

They too came to Jesus of Nazareth with their vehement questions: "When will the kingdom of God come and where is it? Give us some downright, concrete facts and treat us in the same way that men do when they enter into life-and-death partnerships. What we demand of any businessman, indeed, of any honest partner, we demand of you, Jesus of Nazareth. We are not going to fall for any airy castle of a kingdom that nobody has ever seen. We have no intention of staking our lives on a phantom. Either you are a fairy prince, in which case you can go to grandmother and give her something to tell stories about, or you are an

honest, solid partner on whom a man can depend in all
the real, practical, everyday, business affairs of life with
which we men have to deal all the time. So, tell us, Jesus of
Nazareth, where is your kingdom, when is it coming?"

Jesus' answer to that question was very strange and certainly, at first glance, not very satisfying: "Nor will they
say, 'Lo, here it is!' or 'There!'" Why did he reply in just
this way? Was he trying to evade the painful intrusiveness of
the question? But then he went on and gave them a sudden,
headlong answer: "The kingdom of God is in the midst of
you." And what that means is: The kingdom of God is
where I am.

What a long face these people must have pulled when
he said that!

Some of them would have said in their hearts: Well, I
don't see anything "in our midst." All I see is a man who
has a mysterious knack of getting people to follow him, and
undoubtedly has had a good influence on some of them.
That's plain to be seen. Perhaps this man has succeeded in
touching a spiritual chord in these people, a chord which I
don't have. Perhaps in some mysterious way he has been
able to mobilize the mental potentialities of these people, so
that now they think he is their Redeemer, whereas in reality
they are only sustained by their own energies and are therefore victims of an optical illusion.

This type of person, who sees nothing, is always to be
found among the fellow travelers of Jesus and his church.
He is right here among us. These are the people who see
at work in the church certain religious forces or even certain
sociological community-building laws. They see certain historical effects which have emerged from this remarkable
phenomenon called the "Christian church." But really and
truly they see nothing of the reality of a kingdom of God.
Even Pontius Pilate, who certainly recognized the value of
Jesus' personality, and the Roman emperors, who had some
idea of the danger in the power of Christianity to build

community, did not have the vaguest notion of the reality of this kingdom of God which had appeared in Jesus Christ. Otherwise they would not have condemned and executed but, rather, worshiped and adored.

Well, what is the meaning of this assertion of Jesus: The kingdom of God is where I am? Who is this "I"? These people shake their heads in bewilderment. The church of Jesus has always been accompanied by those who shake their heads, and will be until the day of judgment. And frequently enough, it is not always the worst people, humanly speaking, who do not understand.

But then, beside these people, are the others. They prick up their ears when Jesus says, "The kingdom of God is in the midst of you, just as surely as *I* am standing here in the midst of you." Perhaps these others *also* had been thinking: If you are going to talk about a kingdom, then you must also be able to show some clear-cut positions of power, then you have to prove your authority, then you have to be able to say in the clearest possible way: Look here, look there, there it is.

But at this point they are pulled up short. There is, of course, nothing that can be seen or filmed; but what may not be *behind* it? Who is this Jesus, and what is he doing, that he should so incomprehensibly identify his own presence and activity with the presence of the kingdom of God?

And because they stop to think in this way and then fix their eyes steadily upon him, they see that he not only heals sick and crippled bodies but also liberates consciences. They see how people go away from him totally different from what they were before they came. They see that he does not merely challenge people to screw themselves up into some high spiritual state or to engage in complicated devotional exercises or spiritual starvation cures in order to be able to see God. Rather, they observe with amazement that Jesus condescends to the lowly and the poor, and that he is always to be found in the lowermost places of the world. Manifestly, his purpose in all this is to demonstrate that this is what his Father is like. And the fact is that God did send his Son through the back door of the world, through the stable of Bethlehem. He sent him into the darkness of the earth and let him descend into the deepest pits of human suffering and death. So if you want to see God, you don't lift your eyes to the clouds, as is often portrayed in sentimental pictures of prayer, but rather you must look down. God is always in the depths.

And because they are at least perplexed by all this, which is so strange and unaccustomed to them (even unaccustomed in the religious sphere!) and suddenly find it impossible to turn away and pass up the bargain, they find out still more.

They find, as they look into those unearthly eyes, that suddenly they themselves become people who are aware of how much they are lacking; aware of their frailty and the death they must die and their tremendous need for someone who is stronger than the doom of death; aware that they are men with burdened consciences and an urgent need for someone who will break the chains of their guilt and their secret bondages; aware that they are men who think of the future with misgivings and anxious questions and yearn for a king who will hold our times (and therefore the uncertain future time) in his hands.

And because as they look into his eyes they become men who hunger and thirst (for actually this is what they have become—naked, poor in spirit, standing there with empty hands) they suddenly see that he is able to give all this to them, and even that *he* himself is the way to the Father and peace of heart, the power that conquers death, the love that gives a new beginning to all life. Then all of a sudden they see that the kingdom of God actually has begun in him. They see in him the beginnings of what God will show forth in glorious fulfillment on that great day when he will be all in all and the old world will crumble away and a new heaven and a new earth will rise from the flickering flames of the ruins.

I say: *They recognize the kingdom of God only as they recognize the Lord Christ and themselves in him.*

That's why it is that the mystery of the kingdom of God can never be recognized from the outside, by a disinterested spectator, but only from within, by entering into it, in other words, by looking into the eyes of Jesus Christ. That is to say, in the kingdom of God everything is a matter of perspective; everything depends upon where you stand. If you stand at the wrong place, you see absolutely nothing. On the other hand, if you stand at the right place, then even children, fools, and the despised of this world can see the great mysteries of the kingdom of God.

It is like the colored windows of a church. If you go around the outside of the church, you see nothing but gray monochrome and cannot tell whether they are merely dirty, sooty panes or works of art. In other words, you are seeing them from the wrong perspective. But the moment you enter the nave of the church, the windows begin to shine and the whole story of salvation, captured in color, rises up before you. The mystery of the kingdom of God can be seen only if we are "in" it.

That's why Pontius Pilate never discovered who Jesus was. That's why he had only a scornful, and perhaps behind the scorn, a sad smile when Jesus said, "My kingdom is not of this world." Because he did not stand "beneath" the eyes of Jesus, as one who sought his forgiveness and was ready to call him "Lord," he had no "eye" for the kingdom of God, no sense of its proportions. Therefore he had to measure it by his own political standards, compare it with the Roman imperium, and so he saw—nothing. For where were the armies and the ensigns of this kingdom? Where were the more than twelve legions of angels which supposedly would do his bidding? Pontius Pilate saw and heard nothing.

But the harlots who returned to bow before the eyes of Jesus, the poor in spirit whom he had comforted, the children on whose heads he laid his hands, they knew his secret. And they are ready to sell everything to possess the one pearl of great price. And for the mature among them even the splendor of the Roman imperium was only a tawdry bauble, for suddenly they had seen the amplitude of God's kingdom and they knew who would be King when history came to an end.

So we begin to understand why time and again Jesus spoke of the *mystery* of the kingdom of God: From the wise and understanding of this world it is hidden, but to the children and the simple who love him it is revealed. So he speaks of the hidden pearl, the treasure buried in the field, and the secret, unnoticed growth of the kingdom. Everything depends upon where one stands. From our "normal" stance, it is in fact invisibly hidden.

So when we come to the last sentence of the Lord's Prayer: "For thine is the kingdom and the power and the glory," it is not (as we may have thought at first) as if we were given a solid, tangible reason why we can pray all these petitions. It is not as if we had to begin by saying "Our Father" in blind faith and then at the end receive a clear and logical "explanation" which would make faith somewhat easier for us.

No, it is the other way around. First we must learn to speak with our Father. And that may take a long time, perhaps a whole lifetime of praying the Lord's Prayer. We must learn to stand as it were by the side of our brother Jesus, who is praying along with us, testing this prayer and learning from experience that he really does give us our daily bread and forgive us our sins and really can give us a new heart, a heart that is able to forgive others—*before* it begins to dawn on us that we have a Lord who is rich and good and generous and inexhaustible beyond all measure, whose is "the kingdom and the power and the glory." In other words, we never learn how mighty and glorious he is unless we are constantly making demands upon his power and his glory, and thus learning that we never reach the bottom. It might be said that the closing words of the Lord's Prayer are not an *assumption* which we must have accepted in order to be able to pray, but rather the final *conclusion* to which our repeated use of the Prayer has driven us. The last sentence of the Lord's Prayer is therefore a doxology, a paean of praise to God which must break forth from us all when we are overwhelmed by the goodness of God, who is able to do far more abundantly than all that we ask or think.

The Revelation to John helps us to understand the deepest meaning of this doxology. Just as the man who prays the Lord's Prayer, when he comes to the end of his petitions and the thousandfold answers God gives to them, cannot help but burst out in praise of God (and just as the worship of many congregations culminates in this song of praise), so the everlasting praise of angels and the redeemed resounds at the end of *history*. The kingdom of God is the place where the eternal liturgy is sung, the place of unceasing praise to God.

The Christian community has always looked to this end of the ways of God. It is worth noting, in the letters of Paul, for example, that the gaze of Christians turned away from the Christ who walked on earth, or in any case did not dwell upon him, but rather turned to the far more decisive fact— the *coming* Christ. From this view of the end of all the ways of God, the church gains its secret strength and its consolation in the midst of the trials it must endure in the brief interim of ongoing history. The church of Jesus is a company of people who lift up their heads because the old has passed away, because they have caught a glimpse of something coming from the other side.

The way in which this view of history impinges upon our life becomes clear in that very remarkable account in the Book of Acts in which Paul and Silas are thrown into prison after a severe beating and at midnight sing praises to God (Acts 16:25).

What is the secret of this midnight praise that Paul strikes up, of all places, in the darkness of his prison? Is he feeling wonderful? Is he having one of those lyrical moments when he simply must express in words the exultation of his heart? Oh, no! His back is raw and sore from the whiplash, his feet are fastened in the stocks, and the air is damp and oppressive; and he may also have been tormented by the thought of what would happen to the church if God allowed its leader to be snapped up by the police and reduced to silence. Paul's body and spirit are hemmed in on every side by torment.

Nevertheless, he praises God instead of moaning or even (as *we* would likely do) instead of clenching his teeth.

Why?

To praise God means to see things from the perspective of their end, to view them in the light of the great goals and fulfillments of God. *That's* why Paul could sing at midnight, despite his torn and heavy spirit. That's why he could not help but sing, for he knew that if in all his physical and mental pain, he simply dared to praise God—despite the obvious circumstances, despite his reason and his nerves— this end of the ways of God would rise up within his soul and the kingdom of God would surround him in the midst of the damp, dark dungeon.

If there are any among us who are at their wit's end, they ought to try for once to put aside all their grievances and perhaps even all their petitions and simply *praise* God, in order to turn their hearts to the end of the ways of God, where the eternal liturgy resounds in heaven. Nothing so changes us—precisely in the darkest moments of life—as the praise of God. I know a man who by his own calm composure is able to inspire peace in many other people, and was able to do this in the most difficult and feverish times of the bombing war. One day he told me his secret: In the most frightful moments of an air raid he stopped praying to

God and continued only to praise him. That lifted him clean above the spell of these ghastly moments and, looking beyond these seconds of mortal terror, he saw the vast expanse of eternity and the end of the ways of God. Against that background these anguished seconds were nothing more than a swiftly passing moment, and his thoughts rose high above five alarms and gained a whole new perspective.

So, to praise God means to see things from the perspective of the end of things.

We can praise a man only when we have seen what he accomplishes. But we must praise God in order to see what he accomplishes. And therefore we should praise him at the very moments in life when there seems to be no way out. Then we shall learn to see the way out for our own lives, simply because God is there at the end of every way and every blind alley.

So the Lord's Prayer begins with a praiseful appeal to the Father in heaven and closes with the praise of him whose is "the kingdom and the power and the glory." Thus everything we pray for is fenced and enclosed with praise.

Only he who enters this room of prayer can also learn to pray and ask aright. For then he no longer prays under the pressure of the moment and with the shortsightedness of momentary distress, but rather in the light of eternity. He prays from the perspective of the end of the ways of God and so acquires a right sense of the proportions of the kingdom of God, a sense of what is really great and really small.

He sings the hymn of praise: "From God and through God and to God are all things!" And he never ceases to pray:

> O light eternal, fall
> Into this world of time,
> That all things small
> May small abide,
> And all things great
> Be magnified!

But the greatest of all is the Father, whom we learn to know in Jesus Christ. And the smallest is my own self, from which I am freed in Jesus Christ.

All this we are taught by the prayer that spans the world.